About life

that's worth living
and lasts forever

David Mansfield

Introducing Jesus from John's Gospel

First published in Australia in 2001 by
David Mansfield
25 Appletree Place, Menai NSW 2234

All Scripture quotations are taken from the Holy Bible: New International Version. Copyright © 1973, 1978, 1984 by International Bible Society.

National Library of Australia
Cataloguing-in-Publication data

Mansfield, David 1951-
About life: that's worth living and lasts forever
Introducing Jesus from John's Gospel

ISBN 0 957 9873 0 7

1. Bible, NT John
2. Christian life

Edited by Mamie Long
Cover design by Joy Lankshear
Typeset by Barbara Richards
Printed by McPherson's Printing Group

Contents

Before We Start

I was twelve years old when I first holidayed at the Great Barrier Reef in Australia's tropical north. On that visit I viewed this natural wonder of the world from the water's surface in a 'glass-bottom' boat. I was spellbound by its beauty.

On visits since I have been able to 'snorkel' different spots on the Reef, enjoying that beauty at closer range. On my last visit I did some diving, spending long periods of time up close and personal.

I hope your reading of this book will be like my experience of the Reef. As I introduce you to Jesus Christ, I trust that you will be drawn again and again to the wonder of his character and the nature of his claims.

This book, like any other, may be read in one or a few reading sessions. If that is the way you like to read, then go for it and enjoy!

However, if you keep it beside your bed, pack it with your lunch, or have it in a handy place, you may be able to read a short section or a chapter each day or at regular times.

A feature of the book is the way it follows closely what is written in another book called *John's Gospel*. It is one of the books of the Bible that records specific details of the life and teaching of Jesus.

My hope is that you may get hold of a copy of an 'easy to read' Bible if you don't already have one. Then you can read through the whole of John's Gospel and other parts of the Bible at your leisure.

The books of the Bible are divided up into 'chapters' and 'verses'. These act as reference points so that we may easily locate the things that are actually recorded.

I constantly refer to parts of John's Gospel and to other parts of the Bible from time to time. If I say,"John 3:16", for example, it means I am referring to the book of the Bible called John. The '3' stands for the chapter number and the '16' stands for the verse in that chapter.

I have looked at two main sections of John's Gospel. Chapters 1 to 12 of John's Gospel which deal with the three years of Jesus public life, and Chapters 18 to 21 of the Gospel which focus on Jesus' death and resurrection.

I haven't covered Chapters 13 to 17 of John's Gospel which recall the events on the night before Jesus death. I hope to write another book about these chapters.

I became a Christian when a friend introduced me to Jesus Christ and his claims about life. He did this by showing me what Jesus said and did from John's Gospel. That is why John's Gospel was written and why it is very special to me.

John's Gospel has been described like a pool in which a child may wade or an elephant can swim. May it be for you what it has been and continues to be for me.

Like the clear, blue waters of the Great Barrier Reef.

PART ONE

BEGINNING ABOUT LIFE

Chapter 1 shows how our dreams and hopes about life are different from our experience. The promise of Jesus about a 'life in all its fullness' comes with a freshness and relevance that attracts our eager attention.

Chapter 2 looks at John's purpose in writing his Gospel, that we may truly know who Jesus is, come to genuine faith in him, and receive this gift of life.

Chapters 3 and 4 take us to the start of the Gospel where John introduces Jesus to his readers and opens up many of the themes of the Gospel.

1

About Life

Ask an Australian to describe the perfect life and most of us would throw in lots of sun, water and our favourite holiday spot. It's no secret that our country has been dubbed the land of the long weekend!

A young Australian schoolgirl told me that she and a friend came up with an idea one morning before school. They would run away from school and home to experience the perfect life. Their 'blue heaven' would include a beach penthouse with endless days of sunshine. Best of all there would be no teachers to tell them when to stop talking and no parents to tell them when to go to bed. Just 'rule-free' and 'talk-fest' luxury for the rest of their life!

When I asked what became of the grand plan, she replied, "Wouldn't you know it? The school bell rang and we had to go to class!"

The school bell always rings

Dreaming of life as a kind of perfect and permanent holiday is not just a childhood fantasy. Haven't we all caught ourselves wistfully imagining a life made up of our 'perfect day/perfect place' wish list?

The Queensland Tourism Board ran a series of very

successful television commercials with the claim: "Queensland. Beautiful one day. Perfect the next." They got more than they bargained for. Sun-starved Australians from the chilly south migrated in droves for friendlier skies, looking for the 'perfect life'.

Humanity longs for a better life. This deep yearning is common to us all. We love life and the things that make it worth living. We want a long life and an enjoyable life. Not quantity without quality—both.

When things aren't going well we ache for life to be better. Even when things are running fairly smoothly, we have a nagging fear that it can't last. We've been around long enough to know that the school bell always rings.

Basic motivation

But we climb out of bed. We push on. We live in hope. Our thoughts and activities are directed to finding or tightening our grip on a better quality of life.

This single goal determines whether we save or spend, and what we spend our money on. It is why some people stay in dreary jobs for years of their life and why others change theirs repeatedly, to search for something they hope will be more satisfying.

A parent will work long hours. Others will work two jobs. Many parents will both work and overwork the treadmill. Why? To give their kids and themselves what they think will be a better quality of life.

Driven by the same motivation, other parents will work shorter hours, choose less demanding jobs and forgo career moves to spend more time with, and give a better quality of home life to, their kids.

It's universal. We all love life and will do anything in an attempt to add to its length and deepen its quality.

Why can't the good things last?

We long for the good times to keep rolling. We want good things to last. But we know they don't.

Life pushes irresistibly in one direction, with just a little relief and surprise for some. Think back to your last school reunion if you're old enough to have had one.

At my 15 year reunion, many of the 'top' students had their double degrees while some of the 'bottom' students had made their millions! What really struck me was the quiet desperation, the emptiness and the untimely deaths. We were only in our early thirties!

A friend recently shared with me that she was feeling uneasy because her work was keeping her from spending enough time with her two-year-old daughter. I told her that my two year old had just turned twenty-three!

It wasn't the most subtle thing to say, but I needed to be reminded of it as much as anyone.

No wonder the poets in the Bible (this piece is from Psalm 39:4 and 6) say things like:

> **Show me, O Lord, my life's end**
> **and the number of my days;**
> **let me know how fleeting is my life . . .**
> **Each man's life is but a breath.**
> **Man is a mere phantom as he goes to and fro;**
> **He bustles about, but only in vain;**
> **he heaps up wealth,**
> **not knowing who will get it.**

Our view of life

Have you thought much about your view of reality or what life means? Most of the time when we are just cruising we never think of questions like that. But occasionally something will happen that makes us question what meaning life has.

I woke up on Wednesday 12th September 2001 to the news that two hijacked planes had been flown into the towers of the World Trade Centre in New York. Another had taken out a side of the Pentagon in Washington.

Along with the rest of the world I watched in speechless silence. Fuel-laden passenger jets with precious human beings slamming into city skyscrapers and bursting into fireballs. Massive buildings full of working men and women engulfed in flames then collapsing like cards.

Was I awake? Was it folded into a nightmare and morning had not yet come? It seemed unbelievable!

What meaning does life have when it can be treated so savagely? When human life can be taken so brutally? When a person's life can be regarded so cheaply?

What certainties can we hang onto in a world of such uncertainty?

The good and the bad

But it's not just the bad things that make us question the meaning of our lives. It may be a crisis, like the death of a friend, a loved one being struck down with a serious illness or the horrifying events of September 11, 2001.

Or it may be a moment of great happiness like the birth of a child or deep appreciation for the sheer wonder of being alive. It may even be the contradiction of both the good and the bad.

In the movie *Being Human*, Robin Williams plays the role of a divorced father who has weekend access to his two children. He takes them camping and they are sitting around a roaring fire on an isolated beach under a clear night sky.

The father, with feelings of guilt and shame for the way that he has failed his kids, promises them that everything is going to be okay. His teenage daughter knows too well that her father is big on promise but short on delivery so she tries to ease his anxiety and help him enjoy the evening by saying that this may be 'as good as it gets'.

Struggling to accept their pain and yet to enjoy a few moments of pleasure, they gaze at the stars and fall into light-hearted banter about the origin of life and their place in the universe. The father jokes, but with a sense of deep emptiness, that he thinks the universe is like a speck on the skin on a bubble of freshly poured milk!

Here one second and gone the next.

Like a comment I heard on Australian radio by a well-known social commentator who said that humans were about as significant as a grain of sand in a desert. Or actor-director Woody Allen who has said that our lives have as much meaning as waves crashing on the beach.

Views of life in tragic reality

This tragic view of life is played out at a deeply personal level by young Australians and people across the world every day.

I read an all too common article in a Sydney newspaper on the terrible epidemic of youth suicide in this country. A young man, aged about 17, from an Australian regional city was interviewed as he was walking aimlessly on the edge of town. His wrists were scarred from an attempt to end his life. His throat was still red and tender from another. This is how he expressed his feelings about his existence:

This is a shitty little town. This is a big redneck

town. Blokes don't cry. Blokes don't share their feelings. Is this all I was meant for? Just to smoke pot and hang around for the rest of my life?

Does life have more value than this?

Have we more worth than a grain of sand in a windswept desert? Are we really just like waves crashing and disappearing on a lonely beach or a particle on a bubble of freshly poured milk?

Can it get any better than this?

There was an advertisement for a brand of beer that ran on Australian television a couple of years back. It pictured the Bush Tucker Man (a kind of politically correct version of the old Marlboro Man) sitting next to a roaring fire.

It's a typical Australian outback setting under a big night sky. The scene is complete with his 4x4 in a formidable pose in the background. This solitary figure, with a 'cold one' in hand, leans forward and claims, "It doesn't get any better than this!"

But it's a lie. Being on our own is the pits for one thing! If we like it best on our own, we've been hurt or abused in the past. We aren't built to be on our own.

It's also a lie because good times never last. The fire burns down. The wood runs out. The past catches up. Bills have to be paid. Life has to be lived in the cut and thrust of relationships and responsibilities.

What the cameras don't show is the morning after, complete with hangover and tired bones dragging around to clean up the campsite and race off to the next deadline—whether it's back to the dreary job on Monday morning, to see the solicitor on Tuesday or to book the 4x4 in for a service on Wednesday.

A challenge to life as it is

But for a simple, singular claim by Jesus Christ, this could be the end of the story. We could be left with the cruel, cold reality that this is as good as it gets.

There is however a voice of hope. Christianity claims that God has stepped into our world in the person of his Son, Jesus Christ. In John chapter 10 and verse 10 (John 10:10), Jesus clearly and confidently claimed:

> **I have come in order that you may have life, and have it to the full.**

This book is about exploring that claim.

John 20:30-31

Jesus did many other miraculous signs in the presence of his disciples, which are not recorded in this book. But these are written that you may believe that Jesus is the Christ, the Son of God, and that by believing you may have life in his name.

2

About Jesus

Early on in high school my younger daughter started a science project in this way:

> Dear (Science Teacher), I would just like to draw your attention to the fact that no member of my family has a background in the sciences . . . and I think you should take this into account when you mark my project.

You may feel the same way about Christianity as Kim felt about science. You may be thinking, "Never had much to do with church and stuff in the past," or, "Been to a few weddings and a funeral but didn't really listen to what was being said," or, "Guess I've been too busy to check it out."

Whatever our background

This book is for people who haven't had much of a chance to look into Christianity and discover what it's all about. You may have had some negative encounters with church or with 'religious people' and that has been a real 'turn off'. Or you had it rammed down your throat by some well-meaning but 'pushy' person.

But perhaps you've known some impressive people who are Christians. They've caught your eye and made you wonder whether there's something to it after all.

Besides it doesn't go away. Things happen to us. We want answers to the big questions. My hope is that you will put the big questions to the test as we take a look at Jesus' claims about himself and about life.

The source

There are four books of the Bible called Gospels. (The word Gospel simply means 'great news'.) They are historical records of the life and claims of Jesus Christ.

The fourth of these books is John's Gospel. It is the source for what I will say about Jesus. I want you to see that what I'm saying about Jesus isn't made up. I haven't pulled it out of thin air.

In John's Gospel we are going straight to the source of Christianity. To its founder—Jesus Christ. John, a disciple (which means 'follower') of Jesus, calls himself an eyewitness of Jesus' life, death and resurrection. At the end of the Gospel (John 21:24) he says:

> **This is the disciple who testifies to these things, and who wrote them down. We know that his testimony is true.**

The words 'witness' and 'testimony' are key terms in the Gospel of John. We'll come across them often. They have the force of someone under oath in a court of law to tell the truth exactly as they saw it and heard it.

On my way to class one day as a college student I witnessed an accident on a busy highway. I stayed around to lend assistance. As it was getting sorted out the police officer asked me if I would be willing to come down to the station and make a signed statement as an eyewitness. I gladly agreed because I was concerned for the truth of the situation to win out.

John's Gospel is just like that. A kind of 'statutory declaration'; a statement of evidence under oath. John is 'telling the truth, the whole truth and nothing but the truth'.

We have an overwhelming number of these 'eyewitnesses'. John is one of many. After Jesus was raised from the dead he appeared to over 500 people on one occasion. What John said could have been checked out with many others.

Near the end of his Gospel (20:30-31), John tells us why he wrote about Jesus:

> **Jesus did many other miraculous signs in the presence of his disciples which are not recorded in this book. But these are written that you may believe that Jesus is the Christ, the Son of God, and that by believing you may have life in his name.**

I want to pick up three themes that we will meet again and again as we read the Gospel of John. Christianity is all about these three things. It's about **Jesus**. It's about **life**. It's about **trust.**

It's all about Jesus

Jesus Christ is the heartbeat of Christianity. First and foremost, Christianity is about Jesus. He is its subject. He is its substance. The Old Testament section of the Bible points to him. It flows towards him. The New Testament section pivots on him. It flows out from him.

Does this seem so obvious that it hardly needs to be

said? Too often the obvious gets overlooked, or even ignored. Many people have tried to shift the centre of Christianity away from Jesus and onto something else. Usually to some human achievement or focus. Don't miss it—authentic Christianity is all about Jesus.

But be careful! There are lots of strange ideas floating around about who Jesus is. Many years ago a friend of mine was sent to Sunday School for the first time. He was about nine. The teacher asked the class what they knew about Jesus. He shot up his hand and said, "That's the word Daddy uses to make the tractor go!"

Most views about Jesus won't be that crass. But whatever ideas we've picked up about Jesus; from art, songs, movies; from school or university or even from Sunday School or religious 'rellies'; these ideas need to be worked over and changed in the light of what Jesus himself says and does.

Our 'rescuer-king'

John says that Jesus is God's promised 'rescuer-king'. This is the meaning of the word 'Christ' or 'Messiah'.

A king is someone who has the right to rule the lives of others. Good kings serve their people by ruling them lovingly, providing for their needs and protecting them from danger. Jesus' kingship is universal and perfect.

A rescuer is someone who saves the life of another. Life is far less than we would want it to be, let alone what God created it to be. Things in life aren't right. The world's a mess. Suffering and death stink. We long to know our Maker. If only things could get fixed up.

Writer C. S. Lewis in his book *Mere Christianity* described our world as enemy occupied territory and wrote that Christianity is the story of how the rightful king has come to rescue the world from the mess it's in!

Son of God, Lord and God.

John also tells us that Jesus is the **"Son of God."** He has come from God, the Father. He is God's one and only Son. Together they have reached out to rescue the planet.

We are also introduced to the Jesus who is Lord and God. In John 20:24-29, Thomas, one of Jesus' followers, stands face to face with the one whom he saw put to death. Thomas demands hardcore evidence that Jesus had conquered death. Thomas gets what he asks for. Jesus in full, living flesh and blood stands before him. He acknowledges Jesus as **"My Lord and my God."**

This is the Jesus we will meet in John's Gospel. Not Jesus, the swear word. Not the stained glass or the big screen Jesus with blue eyes and perfect skin. Nor the Jesus who many regard as just a 'good teacher' or wonderful model of love and sacrifice.

John's Gospel introduces us to Jesus who is Lord and God. Jesus who is the Son of God. Jesus who is God's promised rescuer and king.

It's all about life

How is it possible to be alive but still need a life?

Life is offered in the name of Jesus. So in some sense there must be a life that we don't have, that we need, and that only Jesus can give.

We were created to live a perfect life. To live in a perfect universe. To enjoy perfect relationships—perfect relationship with our Creator and with each other. But life isn't like that. It's far less than the life that God, in his love and generosity, planned and created us for.

When we plan a holiday, we want two things. Good

weather in a peaceful or exciting place, and to enjoy it with people we get on well with. Same thing when we dream about where we would prefer to live.

My perfect holiday is to be up the coast with my family and mates, enjoying the surf and a few other simple pleasures.

My perfect life sees me in a quiet sub-tropical valley, not far from the ocean. I'm farming a few hectares on a small coastal river.

I can see myself now. It's late in the day and I'm sitting under a mango tree just above the riverbank. The setting sun is brilliant red and a platypus frolics in the water below. I'm up to my armpits in mango juice and rambling on to one of my grandchildren, listening wide-eyed to my stories, before we enjoy dinner on the wide cool verandah of the old cedar homestead.

The details might be different for you, but the general drift will be the same for all of us. Life equals good living! Good place. Good relationships.

But life's not like that. We have one-liners like; 'get a life', and worse; 'life sucks', but worst of all; 'life's a bitch and then you die'.

The Bible talks about our life without God as a kind of death. It's called spiritual death. Even the idea of being alive physically, but in a real sense being dead to true life, isn't all that strange to us. Again we have expressions like; 'I feel like death warmed up' and 'living death'.

Why is life like this? We can trace it back to our rebellion against God. We are cut off from him. This makes us dead spiritually. That deadness, like a virus, has spread to every part of our lives. And death itself will finally get us.

But Christianity is all about life. John's Gospel holds out the hope that Jesus has come to fix that broken relationship with God. Spiritual life instead of spiritual death. A quality of life grander than we could imagine!

Not just 'good relationships/good place'. But our relationship with God fixed. Ultimately life in a perfectly restored universe, enjoying perfect relationships!

It's all about trust

John says that his purpose in writing is so people will 'believe' (the truth about Jesus) and that 'by believing' will receive life (John 20:31).

Trust is to believe or have faith that someone will deliver what they promise by their word, or their character.

John shows us what he means by believing or trusting in Jesus. Thomas stands before the risen Jesus.

Nobody rises from the dead. Unless you can create life. Unless you are God. When Thomas sees Jesus, with life surging through his once lifeless body, Thomas says, **"My Lord and my God."**

In his response Thomas becomes our model of true and genuine trust. This is what it means to believe in Jesus. To honour him as our Lord and our God.

Christianity is all about Jesus, all about life, all about trust.

With this in mind, let's go to the start of the Gospel.

John 1:1-9

In the beginning was the Word, and the Word was with God, and the Word was God. He was with God in the beginning. Through him all things were made; without him nothing was made that has been made. In him was life, and that life was the light of men. The light shines in the darkness, but the darkness has not understood it.

There came a man who was sent from God; his name was John. He came as a witness to testify concerning that light, so that through him all men might believe. He himself was not the light; he came only as a witness to the light. The true light that gives light to every man was coming into the world.

3

About Creation

The Blue Mountains is a world heritage area on the western edge of Sydney. Famous for the 'Three Sisters' rock formation, it boasts some spectacular valley scenery and challenging walking tracks.

Most of these walks begin from a high point on a cliff, where the track plunges into the valley below, and finish with a steep climb out to another cliff top.

As the walk begins you can take in the vast panorama of the valley that you will soon trek through and the distant destination that you will eventually reach.

The opening section of John's Gospel is just like that view from the first cliff top. John lays before his readers the magnificent panorama of the whole book with glimpses of all the themes that he will develop throughout the Gospel.

The God who communicates

John begins his Gospel (John 1:1-2) in this way:

> **In the beginning was the Word, and the Word was with God, and the Word was God. He was in the beginning with God.**

The 'Word' is a person, described as 'He'. It is a name or a title for Jesus. John, in 1:14, says, **"the Word became flesh and made his dwelling among us."**

It's an unusual title. Like a nickname or a special name. You've probably had a number of nicknames in your time. A special pet name that a loved one has given you or a light hearted 'keep you down to size' name that a mate has called you and it has stuck. These names usually point to some feature of your appearance or something about your personality.

Jesus is the 'Word' because in the person of his one and only Son, God speaks to us. In 1:18 John says:

> **No-one has ever seen God, but God, the One and Only, who is at the Fathers side, has made him known.**

The whole of the Bible is God's word to us. In the Old Testament God speaks to us leading up to the coming of Jesus. The New Testament is God speaking to us through Jesus.

Who seeks whom

We are presented with dramatic TV documentaries and magazine articles called things like; *The Search For God* and *The Quest for God*. They give the impression that it is next to impossible to find out anything about God.

They leave you with the idea that if the greatest minds in this world keep on making and producing documentaries, we may just discover a trace or get a sniff of God somewhere. So stay tuned!

If we strike it lucky, we may get a scrap of information. Not much, but just enough to keep us in the hunt. Curious, guessing and good for the show's ratings!

Our family lived for a few years in a rambling old house where every room had at least two doors. It was a great house for playing 'hide and seek' with the kids.

I would hide in a room and listen for the next-door room to be searched and then enter that room by another door. I'd then be sure never to be found in the already searched room and the kids would surrender in a cry of frustration. It was a lousy trick.

Playing hard to find

Slogans like; 'the truth is out there' and 'the search for God' imply that God is mean-hearted and distant. He doesn't really want to be found. To make matters worse he leaves clues around, to tease rather than to help us.

The Gospel of John says that nothing could be further from reality. Jesus is the 'Word'. God speaks and speaks again in the person of his Son.

The God who created words and language has chosen to communicate! The God who could have kept us from knowing him if he chose to, has chosen to reveal himself. Not in teasing half clues but clearly, completely and conclusively in the person of Jesus.

Wherever our search begins, it leads to and ends with Jesus. This is reinforced by the work of John the Baptist. (A different John to the writer of the Gospel.) We read in 1:8-9:

> **(John the Baptist) was not the light; he came only as a witness to the light. The true light that gives light . . . was coming into the world.**

John the Baptist is the last in a long line of Old Testament prophets who pointed to the coming of Jesus.

The God who creates

Before he was born into the world, the Son of God was always there. As we read further into the Gospel we discover that God is three persons: Father, Son and Spirit, in a relationship of perfect love for all eternity.

In the very first chapter of the Bible, in the book called Genesis, we learn that God created by speaking! That's another reason why Jesus is called 'the Word'. He is our Creator. In John 1:2-3 we learn:

Through him all things were made; without him nothing was made that has been made.

The eternal Son of God, in perfect relationship with God the Father and equally God himself, lies at the heart of all God's creative work.

The New Testament fills out the detail of this. All things have been created *through* and *by* Jesus. All things *belong* to Jesus and He is the one who *holds* the universe together (Colossians 1:15-17 and Hebrews 1:3).

Who owns whom

Jesus Christ is our God—our Maker and our Owner. The Bible often uses the word *Lord*. Jesus Christ is Lord. This is why Jesus accepted the response of Thomas (in 20:29) of **"my Lord and my God."**

A few years ago a friend and I went skiing with some of our kids to the New South Wales Snowy Mountains. To travel up to a ski resort we rode in a 'Ski Tube', the first train of its type built in Australia.

We jumped into the front carriage and just as the train was about to leave the station two other men joined us. As the train began to make its way up through the mountain I got talking to the older of the two men. He seemed to know a lot about the Ski Tube and our conversation went like this:

"You seem pretty familiar with the Ski Tube."
"I built it."
"Really, you worked on the construction site?"
"No. I built the whole thing!"
"Oh. You were one of the design engineers?"
"Well I was. But the Ski Tube was my idea from the concept to what we're riding on today."

That piece of information changed everything. The tone of our conversation and the way we related to him. For the rest of the trip we hung on his every word as he told us the story of how he came up with the idea, drew up plans, convinced various consortia and raised finance to realise his dream. All the way up the mountain he gave us detailed information about speed, grade, altitude etc. and told us all sorts of construction stories.

There wasn't a thing to be known about the Ski Tube that he didn't know! On that train and for that ride, we were in the presence of its 'creator' and it was a great experience. To think that when he jumped into 'our carriage' at the station I had resented his intrusion.

Jesus Christ is the Creator, the Designer, the Builder of the universe. He is the 'life-giving' Creator of the world in which we live, of every good thing in life that we have. He is our Creator God. He is the Author of our life!

To know Jesus Christ is to know the God who gave us our last breath and has the power to give or to withdraw our next breath! To know Jesus is to know the God who has given us our life and every good thing in life.

The very possibility that we may know God in a real and personal way should fill us with awe and excitement.

The Creator of relationships

John tells us in 1:4 that Jesus is our 'life-source'.

> **In him was life and that life was the light of men.**

John is not just saying that Jesus has created humanity along with everything else. He has already made that point clear in chapter 1:2-3. The word he uses for 'life' here means our 'spiritual' life. It means life in relationship with God. John is saying that Jesus has created us for this special kind of life as God's friends.

Time Magazine (September 1995) ran an article about a new science called *Evolutionary Psychology*. The article was entitled *The Age of Despair*. It examined the increasing loneliness people are experiencing in the western world at a time when they seem to have everything. The writer said:

> We are designed for trusting relationships and designed to feel uncomfortable in their absence.

I nearly fell off my chair. You would normally use words like 'random' and 'chance' with a science called *Evolutionary Psychology*. How sneaky just to slip in the word 'design'. Even more strange, here was a science claiming what the Bible has always told us!

We are indeed designed for trusting relationships. We are personally designed by Jesus Christ. Personally designed, above all, for trusting relationship with Jesus.

We are designed for relationship by him.

We are designed for relationship with him.

This is what spiritual life is. A relationship of trust with our Creator.

It is not a denial of our physical life. It embraces it and celebrates it. Our physical senses and the physical world are gifts from our Creator. Real and wonderful gifts. But spiritual life is bigger. Bigger and more wonderful by far.

Throughout John's Gospel, 'life' and 'eternal life' are to be understood in this way. Jesus says in 17:3:

> **Now this is eternal life; that they may know you, the only true God, and Jesus Christ whom you sent.**

We ache for intimacy. We hunger for relationships to be better. We long to know God. Have you ever wondered why? Here is our answer. We were created to live in relationship. With our Creator. With each other.

God is at the very core of his being *relational.* He is Father, Son and Spirit and he has made us to bear his *relational* image.

John introduces Jesus as the one through whom God speaks to us. The one who is our Creator, Maker and Life-giver. The one we were created to enjoy relationship with.

We need to explore why that relationship is broken.

John 1:10-18

He was in the world, and though the world was made through him, the world did not recognise him. He came to that which was his own, but his own did not receive him. Yet to all who received him to those who believed in his name, he gave the right to become children of God—children born not of natural descent, nor of human decision or a husband's will, but born of God.

The Word became flesh and made his dwelling among us. We have seen his glory, the glory of the One and Only, who came from the Father, full of grace and truth.

John testifies concerning him. He cries out, saying, "This was he of whom I said, 'He who comes after me has surpassed me because he was before me.' " From the fullness of his grace we have all received one blessing after another. For the law was given through Moses; grace and truth came through Jesus Christ. No one has ever seen God, but God the One and Only, who is at the Father's side, has made him known.

4

About Rebellion

Across the world rebellions are a part of life. An elected government is overthrown by a military coup. Dictators are deposed by rebel forces. 2000 AD was the year for coups in the South Pacific. For months a rebel leader held the Fijian cabinet hostage in Government House. His demands were simple. He just wanted to run the country!

Not that all rebellions are bad. History glitters with worthy heroes. People who have led rebellions against evil forces, or taken up the fight against injustice.

What makes rebellion wrong? It depends on answers to these questions: Who does the rebelling? Who is rebelled against? Why have they rebelled?

John's Gospel tells us that we have all rebelled against our Creator. We read in John 1:10:

> **He was in the world, and though the world was made through him, the world did not recognise him.**

Our purpose

Our world **"was made through Jesus Christ"** (1:10). A personal and purposeful God created us. We haven't been coughed up by chance. We are not the result of a cosmic hiccup.

That means life has meaning. History has purpose. Humanity has dignity. We have been carefully, lovingly created. Our Creator is not something, but someone!

It also means that our future can be full of hope. Jesus Christ is our God. We belong to him. We are loved by him. We belong nowhere else but securely inside that good and loving relationship with him that he created us for.

I have never met a person who is not stoked by the sheer beauty and simple pleasures that life offers.

My daughter, Jenny, was on a student exchange, staying in Switzerland, when she was 16. She rang one night bursting with excitement. That day her host family had taken her on a helicopter ride over the Swiss Alps. She witnessed the sun setting behind the Matterhorn.

Or take my surfing trip with some mates for a few days up the coast. Every day we saw or surfed amongst dolphins. On one occasion a whale surfaced no more than 50 metres from where I sat spellbound on my surfboard.

What a great thing to experience some of the delights the creation holds out to us. But what can be greater than the wonder of knowing the love, and enjoying the friendship of the Creator of this life? And to know that his purpose for our life is that very friendship!

Our shame

But John tells us that **"the world did not recognise him"** (1:10). This doesn't mean that Jesus went through life in disguise, keeping his identity under wraps, not wanting to be recognised.

When we moved to the suburb where we now live I was told that one of Australia's elite cricketers lived nearby. But the story was that he always wore dark glasses and a cap in public so he wouldn't be noticed! I didn't know if the rumour was true but for years I never saw him.

Then one day over at the shopping centre, there he was, as large as life. No sunglasses. Just doing the shopping with his wife. Doting over his kid in the stroller. Anyone could have met him and chatted to him. He was easy to recognise.

Jesus came to be recognised. He didn't come wearing dark glasses to avoid us. Just the opposite. He came so that we may know him.

Bad choice

Men and women chose not to recognise or acknowledge who he was. They rejected him. The statement in 1:11 demonstrates this and reinforces the point John is making:

> **He came to that which was his own, but his own did not receive him.**

This is a specific reference to the way the first century Jewish people treated Jesus when he lived among them. They rejected his claim to be their God. Think about the contrast between these realities. It could not be more scandalous.

> **The world was made through him.**
> **The world did not recognise him.**
> and
> **He came to that which was his own.**
> **His own did not receive him.**

But the Jewish rejection of Jesus doesn't let us off the hook. For the way they treated Jesus in the first century is no different from the way that men and women have treated God in every century! Just like the way we have rejected Jesus in our own day.

Shocking contrast

In the movie *Good Morning Vietnam* a stark contrast is crafted on screen to drive home the shock and shame and scandal of war. The song *What a Wonderful World* plays to scenes of the carnage of war.

We hear lyrics that speak of green trees and red roses in full bloom, but see valleys and villages wasted by bombing raids.

We hear the deep soft tones of Louis Armstrong sing about rainbows and happy smiling faces, but we see young men gunned down in back alleys and violent street clashes between protesters and soldiers.

When I saw that incredible piece of movie making I wondered whether it was possible to have a greater contrast. Until I thought again about John's words.

Here is the greatest of all scandals. The worst of all rebellions. The creation rejecting its Creator! This behaviour lies at the heart of all evil. This is the great shame of humanity. Each one of us is guilty.

From bad to worse

A few years ago when our kids were quite young I had to go away for a few days. When I came home and walked through the front door I was greeted by a scene that would warm the heart of every father. Hanging from one side of the hallway to the other was a huge banner. Written on the banner in big, bold and colourful letters were the words: WELCOME HOME DAD.

My kids came running up the hallway to greet me with big hugs. Behind them came Helen with a look of relief written all over her face.

It was a great moment. I had come home to where I belonged. Home to the people I belonged to, and to the people who belonged to me. And I was welcomed and received as I should have been.

But let's imagine a different scene. Say I walked through the front door only to be greeted by a cold, grey hallway. I can hear the kids playing down in the back of the house so I call out, "Hey guys, I'm home." There's no response. I call out again. Still nothing. All of a sudden the kids come tearing up the hallway, brush past me and off into another part of the house, completely ignoring me. They treat me as if I'm not even there.

Helen appears in the hall. No smile. No welcome. The look on her face freezes my blood. Then in a flat and lifeless voice she says, "I've done some thinking while you've been away. I want you to leave without making a scene. You're not welcome here anymore. In fact all your stuff is packed up out in the shed. I want you to live there so you'll be around to pay the bills and make us feel a bit safer, but that's all!"

How would I have felt? If I had come home to where I belonged and instead of acceptance, I was shoved aside.

In relating to God that is what we've done. Instead of welcoming Jesus as our king we've pushed him out. At times we've even been rude enough to expect him to be 'on call' from the back shed.

Can you see how wrong this treatment of Jesus is? This is what the Bible means by the word 'sin'. We are all in this together and we are all guilty. Each of us has ignored Jesus. We all deserve God's judgment. Unless

God shows mercy to us, our situation is hopeless.

Throughout the Gospel we will see the outworking of this relentless rejection of Jesus by 'his own' people.

Our hope

Is there hope for such behaviour? Let's go back to those words in 1:10: **"He was in the world."**

Now look at what John goes on to say in 1:12-13:

> **Yet to all who received him, to those who believed in his name, he gave the right to become children of God—children born not of natural descent, nor of human decision or a husband's will, but born of God.**

Did you notice the totally unexpected here? Jesus gives people the right to become members of God's family. How can this be? Take a close look at what happens between 1:11 and 1:12. Some people change. They changed their mind about Jesus. They believed in him. They received him. They stopped rejecting him and began to honour and trust him.

What a twist! In shutting out Jesus, we find ourselves shut out. Instead of remaining shut out, we are provided with a way back in.

Hope of belonging

John is again using the language of relationship. The language of family. Knowing God as our 'Father in heaven'. Becoming his child. Belonging.

Life is about being where you belong. The whole point of this book is to demonstrate that we belong nowhere else but securely in that relationship God created us to enjoy with him. That relationship we forfeited through our stupid and pathetic shot at independence.

How do we come home? John's words could not be clearer. We are to receive him. We are to believe in his name.

I live in a part of Sydney that has been ravaged by fierce bushfires in recent years. Out of these tragic fires have come heartbreaking stories of death and grief, but also heart-warming stories of bravery and help.

One of my favourite stories is that of a small boy who was walking beside his parents while they sifted through the charred remains of their family home. A news reporter asked the boy what he was going to do now that he no longer had a home . The boy slipped his hand into his father's hand, looked up at the reporter and replied:

> Oh mister, you've got it all wrong. I may not have a house, but I've sure got a home!

True belonging starts when you slip your hand into the hand of Jesus. Welcoming him into your life as your king. Returning to that relationship you were created for.

That's coming home.

Home to life in all its fullness.

PART TWO

STORIES ABOUT LIFE

Throughout chapters 5 to 13 we look in detail at several stories of the ministry and miracles of Jesus.

John records seven miracles in chapters 2 to 11 of the Gospel. He calls them 'signs'. They point to Jesus' true identity. They truly are 'signs of life'.

The signs are woven into the stories of people who meet Jesus. They encounter the living and life-giving God and through these encounters we meet him too.

He calls upon us to trust him. He promises forgiveness and life.

John 2:1-11

On the third day a wedding took place at Cana in Galilee. Jesus' mother was there, and Jesus and his disciples had also been invited to the wedding. When the wine was gone, Jesus' mother said to him, "They have no more wine."

"Dear Woman, why do you involve me?" Jesus replied. "My time has not yet come."

His mother said to the servants, "Do whatever he tells you."

Nearby stood six stone water jars, the kind used by the Jews for ceremonial washing, each holding from twenty to thirty gallons.

Jesus said to the servants, "Fill the jars with water"; so they filled them to the brim.

Then he told them, "Now draw some out and take it to the master of the banquet."

They did so, and the master of the banquet tasted the water that had been turned into wine. He did not realise where it had come from, though the servants who had drawn the water knew. Then he called the bridegroom aside and said, "Everyone brings out the choice wine first and then the cheaper wine after the guests have had too much to drink; but you have saved the best till now."

This, the first of his miraculous signs, Jesus performed in Cana of Galilee. He thus revealed his glory, and his disciples put their faith in him.

5

About Glory

Does it surprise you that the first miracle Jesus performed is at a wedding? Or that the miracle itself is the production of 600 litres of vintage wine?

It should really come as no surprise that Jesus, the author of life and our life-giver, shows us his glorious character at an occasion that celebrates the wonder and beauty of human life; marriage!

John begins the story of this remarkable day (2:1-2):

> **On the third day a wedding took place at Cana in Galilee. Jesus' mother was there, and Jesus and his disciples had also been invited to the wedding.**

Weddings are exciting but stressful affairs. So much is on show. So much more is at stake. It's a day when it's never more important that everything goes right. When it's never more embarrassing if something goes wrong.

Something goes very wrong at this wedding. It was the responsibility of the bridegroom's family to provide enough drink for the party. Failure to do so was a serious thing in the culture of Jesus' day. It brought social rejection and shame. Legal action was not uncommon.

Here was a family in deep trouble. No bottle shops or pubs to whip down to and fix the situation. No mates to ring on the mobile phone and ask them to help out. They had under-supplied and the fallout would be serious.

The wine runs out (2:3). But Jesus steps in. He changes 600 litres of water into premium quality wine.

His maiden miracle

Why would Jesus perform such an unusual miracle? In John 2:11 we read:

> **This, the first of his miraculous signs, Jesus performed at Cana in Galilee. He thus revealed his glory and his disciples put their faith in him.**

This is not the first time John has used the word 'glory'. Back in 1:14 John says:

> **The word became flesh and made his dwelling among us. We have seen his glory.**

The word 'seen' is a very strong one. It means that the disciples were spellbound by what they saw. They were truly 'gobsmacked'.

Glory is a 'true colours' thing. It's the defining feature that makes someone great. The glory of famous sportspeople is watching them do what they do best and have become famous for. We never tire of seeing them in action.

This miracle reveals Jesus' glory. It points to his true identity and to the life we can have in relationship with him. We are shown this in two ways. Jesus is our life-giving Creator and Jesus is our loving rescuer.

Jesus is our life-giving Creator

What would you say about a person who can change the chemical formula of water so that it becomes a different kind of liquid altogether? And he does this with a simple decision of his mind.

Only our Creator could do it. Jesus demonstrates that he has the power you would link only with God.

In Sydney a few year ago, the NSW Government had to consult with the world's best experts to provide safe drinking water to the city. They needed to fix the problem of a few undesirable bugs in the water to make it drinkable. It took weeks and millions of taxpayers' dollars to bring the problem under control. What they would have given for the power that Jesus had!

But this miracle is much more than a demonstration of raw power. Jesus' character is more glorious than one simple display of power for its own sake. It is his sovereign power used out of love for people.

Like this 'dry' wedding, human life is empty of any real meaning and full of hardship and trouble. It's not the kind of life that a perfect, loving Creator would design.

Tragically, it's the life we have chosen by rejecting him. We are living out the painful consequences of that rejection—insecurity, fears, failure, hurt, emptiness, shame and death.

Is there any hope?

Jesus reveals his glory at a simple village wedding on the verge of disaster. He shows his power. He shows his deep personal concern. He comes to the rescue. In doing so he gives us a glimpse of the relationship he created us to enjoy and the relationship he came to restore us to.

His love for us

Jesus touches the lives of these people in the midst of family celebration. This wedding took place in an outback village in a forgotten province of the Roman Empire. Thousands of such weddings take place across the world every week. They come and go without the slightest notice being taken by anyone other than the invited guests and a clutch of curious onlookers. Why was this wedding different? Only that Jesus happened to be a guest. These people were important to him.

Ordinary people like you and me are important to Jesus. No matter how unimportant you consider yourself to be, you matter to Jesus. Other people may have worked you over and left you feeling like your life is worthless and you don't matter to anyone. Jesus will not, and will never treat you like that!

I've carried a childhood memory with me right through life. There was an unpopular kid in my class when I was in kindergarten. Don invited all the boys in the class to his sixth birthday party. But I couldn't go. During the next week my Mum met his Mum at the shops and asked how the party went. It had been cancelled because nobody could go. The kid was six!

We've all been hurt at some time, been passed over, forgotten, dumped or just ignored. The excuses seemed good at the time. People are busy. A friendship that had come to mean a lot to us, and with no explanation we were just left in the cold. Even within our own family we can been made to feel like we don't belong.

In relationship with Jesus we can be sure of the love of the one who is our life-giving Creator.

His acceptance of us

How must the groom's family have felt when this

wedding was about to unravel? How would they show their faces in public again? The stigma and shame they would have to live with. The gossip and criticism they would have to endure. The muttering and awkward looks as people left the party early.

But when Jesus is alerted to the situation there is no criticism, no sharp remark to heighten their embarrassment, no wisecrack to deepen their humiliation. He quietly swings into action in a remarkable way. He shows his understanding, care and acceptance of people even when they have 'blown' it.

We are rarely treated like this. Mostly we are put down for 'getting it wrong'. Sometimes with a word or just a look. When we've done something stupid we don't need to have it rubbed in. We've probably done the 'putting down' as often as being 'put down'. Jesus will never treat us like that.

In the movie *Awakenings*, a New York doctor has a number of patients in his care who are permanent residents in a public hospital. They have been in a coma for most of their lives due to a childhood disease.

The patients respond to a new drug and are 'awakened' and begin to experience what it means to be 'alive'. They start to enjoy human contact, friendship and many of the simple joys of living.

The doctor asks one of the patients what it was like to be 'awakened'. The two men had become very close friends. The patient responds to the doctor's question:

> "I thought it was a dream at first."
> "When did you realise that it wasn't a dream,"
> asks the doctor.
> "When I spoke and you understood me,"
> answers the patient.

When I spoke and you understood me! To understand and be understood. To love and to be loved. To know and to be known. Jesus shows his glory. Why? So that we may know him and know him properly and intimately. He understands and cares for us with a love, sympathy, compassion and mercy that is perfect and absolute. Even though there is nothing about us that is hidden from him. He accepts us as we are.

Could there be any better news than this? Did you imagine in your wildest dreams that Christianity could be like this? You can't hide from God and you can't hide anything from God. Yet you can't stop God loving you, being for you and wanting to forgive you.

His desire for us

Look at the nature of this miracle. We're told that there are six stone water jars on hand. They are filled to the brim. The water is changed into wine. But not just ordinary wine. Not the wine you would find in a flagon or cask or cheap bottle. The very best quality wine. Wine chosen and kept for the most special moments of the most important occasions.

A friend of mine owns two bottles of a famous Australian wine that fetches several hundred dollars a bottle at auction! Can wine be that good? Jesus gives this family 800 bottles of the very best.

Have you heard people say that they wouldn't become a Christian for fear that they'd have to give up too much or because they might miss out on too much fun? Jesus' action blows that idea clean out of the water.

Back in the Old Testament God describes the promised time of Jesus coming with the picture of a bumper grape harvest when the mountains would flow with limitless amounts of the best wine. The 'mother of all harvests' (Amos 9:13).

Jesus transforms this scene from shortfall to overflow, from need to provision, from shame to celebration.

What does it mean for people who trust Jesus for life? He is not a fun spoiler or a joy killer. Jesus will never use us and then toss us aside.

It's other people who often treat us like that.

Jesus will fill our life with forgiveness and love. He will open up horizons of hope and purpose in life that we never thought could exist.

Jesus is our loving rescuer

Jesus didn't come just to rescue a wedding feast from failure or a family from deep social shame. Nor did he come just to heal sick people and help hurting people. He came to rescue people from every century and from every nation, from the shame, guilt and judgment that our rebellion against God deserves.

He says to his mother in 2:4, **"My time has not yet come."** Along with the word **'glory'** this word **'time'** in John's gospel has its focus on the great rescuing mission for which he came. Always with an eye on that great rescuing work he 'rescues' this family. So this, like every rescuing action in his life, points to the great rescue mission he came to accomplish through his death and resurrection.

Here we have a snapshot or a 'curtain-raiser' of that great work. Of Jesus' power and compassion. Of the change and difference he can bring to life.

John 3:1-8

Now there was a man of the Pharisees named Nicodemus, a member of the Jewish ruling council. He came to Jesus at night and said, "Rabbi, we know you are a teacher who has come from God. For no one could perform the miraculous signs you are doing if God were not with him."

In reply Jesus declared, "I tell you the truth, no one can see the kingdom of God unless he is born again."

"How can a man be born when he is old?" Nicodemus asked. "Surely he cannot enter a second time into his mother's womb to be born!"

Jesus answered, "I tell you the truth, no one can enter the kingdom of God unless he is born of water and the Spirit. Flesh gives birth to flesh, but the Spirit gives birth to spirit. You should not be surprised at my saying, 'You must be born again.' The wind blows wherever it pleases. You hear its sound, but you cannot tell where it comes from or where it is going. So it is with everyone born of the Spirit."

6

About Perspective

There's a great story about a daughter who leaves home to study at university. After a few months, her parents finally receive their first email from her. It goes like this:

Dear Mum and Dad,
I guess you thought I'd dropped off the face of the earth. Sorry I've been so slack in not being in touch but at last I can bring you up to date. But before you read on, please pour yourselves a strong drink and make sure that you're both sitting down! I'm doing okay now. The skull fracture and the heavy concussion I got when I jumped out of the window of my room when the whole of the building caught on fire soon after my arrival here has almost healed. I only spent two weeks in hospital and now I can see almost normally and only get those sick headaches every other day. Thankfully, the fire and my jump were witnessed by a boy who pumps petrol at the 'servo' across the road and he was the one who called the fire truck and the 'ambo'. He also visited me in the hospital and since I had nowhere to live after the fire, he

kindly invited me to share his little flat with him. He is a really nice boy and, well, we have fallen in love and are planning to get married. We haven't set the exact date yet but it will be before my pregnancy begins to show. Yes, Mum and Dad, I am pregnant. I know how much you are looking forward to being grandparents and I know you will welcome the baby and give it the same love and devotion you gave me when I was a child. He is a kind man and although he is of a different race and religion from ours, I know your often expressed tolerance will mean you are not bothered by that.

Now that I have brought you up to date, let me tell you that there was no fire. I have not had concussion. There is no skull fracture. I was never in hospital. I am not pregnant, I am not engaged and there is no boyfriend. However I have failed Biology and History and I want you to see those marks in their proper perspective!

How do we keep life in perspective? What is the proper perspective that we should have anyway?

In the dark

This man who came to see Jesus, called Nicodemus, was a religious leader. He is described as a Pharisee and a member of the ruling Jewish council. He had reached the top of his tree in terms of his status.

These guys were leaders and role models in Jewish society. The people in their communities held them in huge respect. The Pharisees had the job of helping people to keep things in perspective. They were to remind people of what was important in life.

John tells us it was night. The conversation that follows shows that when it comes to spiritual truth this 'spiritual leader' is as much in the dark as the night he steps out of.

This encounter between Jesus and Nicodemus illustrates what Jesus says about the state of the human heart at the end of the previous chapter of the Gospel. In John 2:24-25 we read:

> **But Jesus would not entrust himself to them, for he knew all men. He did not need man's testimony about man, for he knew what was in a man.**

Whose perspective matters?

Nicodemus pays Jesus a polite compliment (John 3:2). I'm sure he saw Jesus as barely more than one among equals, who had no more light to shed on life than the members of his own 'club'—an elite group of men who were never backward in telling people how to live.

There's no shortage of people around today offering advice on how life should be lived and how to keep focused on the things that matter. There is no end of 'self help' books to read and seminars to sign up for.

A lot of this advice is very attractive to a society whose lives have careered out of control with ambition and busyness. Or people feeling brain dead with the boredom of life.

Hence the popularity of TV soapies with their 'back to the bush' and quiet country life themes—carefully spiced with a little sexual tension in each episode.

Sea Change, the Australian TV series, was a huge success with its life by the sea romanticism. Even the title is a commonly used expression for our deep yearning to escape our urban prisons for a simpler life.

In the closing scenes of the movie *Awakenings*, the doctor addresses the hospital medical board on the failure of his project with a group of comatose patients:

> The human spirit is more powerful than any drug. And that's what needs to be nourished. With work, play, friendship, family. The things that matter. This is what we'd forgotten. The simplest things.

Words like these touch us at very tender points. But are they the things that matter most, as attractive and important as they are? What matters most?

Jesus goes straight to the heart of these issues. He shows Nicodemus (3:3) what the real issues of life are:

I tell you the truth, no one can see the kingdom of God unless he is born again.

The kingdom of God

Jesus confronts Nicodemus with the reality of **"the kingdom of God"** and the need to be **"born again"**. To face these issues is to get life in its proper perspective.

The kingdom of God means the rule or the ultimate authority of God. Jesus is the king of this kingdom. He is the one who has the right to rule our lives. We were created to live under this good and loving rule.

I was explaining this to a guide who had just taken a group of us on a white water rafting trip. That night over coffee I talked about Jesus being the king of the universe and his right to rule our lives.

To help him see this we talked about his role as our

rafting guide and his job to get us safely through the dangerous rapids. At the start of the day he drilled several commands into us. We were left in no doubt who was in charge and whose orders we were to obey. We knew too that the orders he gave us were for our good because he cared deeply for our safety and enjoyment!

He could understand that in that raft, on that river, he was king! This was his kingdom. We were his subjects. His orders were to be followed. They were for our good.

I was able to show our guide what would happen if we ignored or disobeyed his orders: if one of us with the backing of 15 minutes experience started to claim we knew better than the guide and another got sick of being told what to do, and we pushed the guide out of the raft—a bizarre kind of mutiny. It would have been comical but tragic. Such action would put all the rafters at grave risk.

We have all done this to Jesus. Jesus is the world's king. He is the rightful king of our lives, but we have rejected him. Our relationship with God is broken.

The second birth

The hope held out to Nicodemus and all of us is that it is possible to **"see the kingdom of God."** We can have a second chance in life. He is offering forgiveness if we come back to him. Enjoying his loving rule over our lives need not be lost forever.

The words Jesus uses to describe this second chance are unusual. Remember he says in John 3:3:

> **I tell you the truth, no one can see the kingdom of God unless he is born again.**

He reinforces it in 3:5 and 7 by saying:

I tell you the truth, no one can enter the kingdom of God unless he is born of water and the Spirit . . . You should not be surprised at my saying, 'You must be born again.'

To be born again means to be born of the Spirit. Jesus is referring to the work of the Holy Spirit. The Holy Spirit causes people to realise that their rebellion against Jesus is wrong. He convicts people of this rebellion, their need to turn back to Jesus, ask for his forgiveness and surrender their lives to his rule.

This 'rebirth' or second birth means that a person who is born physically is now born spiritually. We are first born into a biological family but we need to be born into God's spiritual family.

Once orphans, we can become children in God's family. Once rebels against Jesus' rule, we can be forgiven and become loyal citizens in the kingdom of God.

Our greatest need and only hope

Like Nicodemus, our greatest need is for spiritual birth. Even though he was a religious leader he was doomed to eternal separation from God without it. Even if he thought he had lived a moral life compared to others, unless he submitted to the authority of Jesus he was without hope.

Unless we are born again, we remain spiritually dead. We will never enter the kingdom of God.

Jesus urgently tries to impress the importance of this truth on Nicodemus. He appeals in 3:14-15 to this religious leader's knowledge of his people's history.

Just as Moses lifted up the snake in the desert, so the Son of Man must be lifted up, that everyone who believes in him may have eternal life.

Jesus is reminding Nicodemus of a time when a plague of poisonous snakes was inflicted on God's people as judgment for their disobedience. The only way to be saved from fatal snakebites was to fix their eyes on a pole that God instructed their leader, Moses, to erect with a bronze snake statue mounted on it.

As people raised their eyes to the uplifted snake, in obedience to God's command and provision, he healed them. This showed their sorrow for their disobedience and renewed resolve to obey him. (This is recorded in the Old Testament book called Numbers 21:4-9.)

Jesus refers to himself as the one who would be lifted up, pointing to his death on the cross. As people look to him in trust, they too will be healed of the fatal consequences of sin and rebellion and receive eternal life.

A radical wake up call

Jesus is calling us to a radical 'awakening'. So radical that it's more like a resurrection from death than waking from a coma! That's just what it must be. We are spiritually dead and only the Spirit of God can bring us to life.

To be 'born again' to this spiritual life is the proper perspective on life that Jesus urges us to embrace.

John 4:4-10

Now he had to go through Samaria. So he came to a town in Samaria called Sychar, near the plot of ground Jacob had given to his son Joseph. Jacob's well was there, and Jesus, tired as he was from the journey, sat down by the well. It was about the sixth hour.

When a Samaritan woman came to draw water Jesus said to her, "Will you give me a drink?" (His disciples had gone into the town to buy food.)

The Samaritan woman said to him, "You are a Jew and I am a Samaritan woman. How can you ask me for a drink?" (For Jews do not associate with Samaritans.)

Jesus answered her, "If you knew the gift of God and who it is that asks you for a drink, you would have asked him and he would have given you living water."

7

About Emptiness

What would you list among your greatest fears? Over the years the things that really scare me have changed. Once, the big fear was school exams. Now, it's whether I can survive the week. Sometimes, it's whether I just had my photo taken by a speed camera.

I'm not afraid of heights, water or speaking in front of a group of people, although that still makes me a little nervous. I'm told in most surveys the fear of public speaking polls ahead of the fear of death! To which comedian Jerry Seinfeld quips that people would rather be in the box than giving the eulogy!

Old fears

Now that I'm in my middle years I have to confess that the fear of growing old is a big one. A lady once asked me how many grandchildren I had. "None!" I blurted out, even though I was old enough to have had several! The shock of hearing the question for the first time nearly gave me concussion!

A little later I was on a holiday jogging back from the beach to our rented cottage, I crossed a grassy reserve where a game of touch footy was being played. As I skirted the action, a bloke ran towards me to score a try.

He sidestepped around me and said, "Gee, for a moment there, I thought you were going to tackle me, Old Timer." *Old Timer*! It had been a tough year but I thought I was wearing it better than that.

Deeper fears

But is growing old our deepest fear? What about being passed over by friends? Taken down by people we trusted? Retrenched from a job in which we sweated out the best years of our working life?

Or failure as a parent? Being all but forgotten by adult children? Denied the joy of seeing our grandchildren grow? Being cheated or discarded by our spouse?

Love given but unreturned! This is a deep fear—the unspoken fear that is common to us all.

The song *Will You Still Love Me Tomorrow?* captures the uncertainty and anxiety of the human heart. It cries out for the assurance of genuine love. It expresses the deep fears of many in an age that has sought the pleasure of sex without the responsibility of commitment.

Fear and reality

But what happens when our fears become reality? When our love is given but not returned? When we have no choice but to live with the pain of that reality?

The woman Jesus meets at a village waterhole is no stranger to these fears. In John 4:7-9 Jesus makes what seems to be a simple request:

> **Jesus said to her, "Will you give me a drink." (His disciples had gone into town to buy food.)**
> **The Samaritan woman said to him, "You are a Jew, and I am a Samaritan woman.**

How can you ask me for a drink?" (For Jews do not associate with Samaritans.)

Why is she so surprised? Firstly, Jews and Samaritans hated each other. There was a deep racial and religious rift that went back many centuries. Secondly, Jewish men didn't talk to women in public—even their own wives, let alone a Samaritan woman. And, as we shall see, a woman with a very questionable reputation!

In 4:16-18 we learn that she has had six partners:

He told her, "Go, call your husband and come back."
"I have no husband", she replied.
Jesus said to her, "You are right when you say you have no husband. The fact is, you have had five husbands, and the man you now have is not your husband. What you have just said is quite true."

Imagine what life must be like for a person to have endured that number of failed relationships. Her confidence and trust would have been a shambles.

But there are clues in the story to suggest that this was not the worst of it. It was about midday and the woman was alone when she came to fill her water pot. The women of the village would come in groups and do so in the cool of the early evening.

This woman is on her own in more ways than one. A reputation like hers would make many married women in a small town nervous. Shunned by friends and shamed by a life of relational failure, this burnt out 'love-aholic' comes to the well alone, and at a time when any human contact is unlikely. Her emptiness was very deep.

For some the pain never stops. It may be yours. It may belong to a friend. It is real pain and it hurts.

If what I'm saying doesn't touch you at all; if your life is just one long party, remember that parties don't last and the room is half filled with lonely people anyway.

In the movie *Notting Hill* Julia Roberts plays the part of a famous Hollywood actress who is thought to have a life and life-style that most people would kill for. But in one scene she speaks about her life in this way:

> I'm 29 years of age and I've been on a diet since I was 19 which means that I've been hungry for 10 years. I've had a series of not very nice boys. And every time my heart gets broken the media make a circus out of it. I've had to have two painful operations to look like this and one day I won't be wanted by anyone.

None of us is immune to the emptiness that life can bring. Failure at relationships and our obsession with sex signal the loneliness of much human existence.

Touched by Jesus

Jesus' concern for this woman is characteristic of the Jesus we are meeting and getting to know in John's Gospel. The friendship he offers is for all people (John 2). The spiritual birth he gives is without favour (John 3). The love he shows is regardless of lifestyle, background or race (John 4).

Compare this encounter with the Samaritan woman and the conversation with Nicodemus. He was a leading Jewish citizen. She is a Samaritan peasant. He tried to lead a life of moral integrity. Her life had morally fallen apart.

To Jesus they are of equal importance. He treats them with equal respect. He addresses their common need. To human eyes they may be worlds apart, but in Jesus' eyes they're spiritual twins.

And how does Jesus speak to this woman? With the same directness that he spoke to Nicodemus. He goes straight to the heart of her real need (4:10):

> **Jesus answered her, "If you knew the gift of God and who it is that asks you for a drink, you would have asked him and he would have given you living water."**

The gift of God

Empty lives don't have to stay that way. Jesus speaks of the gift of God. He is the one who gives that gift.

The gift Jesus offers is described as 'living water' (4:10). Like Nicodemus, the Samaritan woman fails to see that Jesus is using picture language to describe spiritual reality (4:11-12). So he spells out the nature of the gift in more detail in 4:13-14:

> **Jesus answered her, "Everyone who drinks this water will be thirsty again, but whoever drinks the water I give him will never thirst. Indeed the water I give him will become in him a spring of water welling up to eternal life."**

Jesus uses the language of common need to speak to the woman about her real need. Her empty life was more important than an empty water pot. She wasn't created for pain and emptiness.

Jesus offers a gift that will satisfy our endless thirst for happiness. A spring of water means abundant supply and continual provision. All we could hope for and more. It will never dry up. It will never run out. He offers himself. He will give his Spirit to those who trust him. In 7:37-39 Jesus says:

"If anyone is thirsty, let him come to me and drink. Whoever believes in me, as the Scripture has said, streams of living water will flow from within him." By this he meant the Spirit, whom those who believed were later to receive . . .

The Son of God

Jesus identifies himself as the giver of this gift. The one whom Nicodemus comes to in the dark of the night. The one whom this woman meets in the heat of the day.

When the Samaritan woman turns to the subject of where people are to worship God (4:19-20), Jesus points her to a time that is fulfilled by his coming.

True worship, and the truth itself, is not found in a place but in a person. Christianity is not a religion but a relationship. In 4:23-24 he says:

Yet a time is coming and has now come, when the true worshipers will worship the Father in spirit and truth, for they are the kind of worshipers the Father seeks. God is spirit, and his worshipers must worship in spirit and truth.

Remember the expression; **"my time"** (John 2:4)? It was the way Jesus spoke about his reason for coming into the world—to die! It will be through his death and only through his death that men and women can come back to God. The only way to know God as Father and honour or worship him as Father is through the Son. To worship him in spirit and truth means to trust and obey his Son.

This talk about true worship prompts the woman to raise the issue of God's 'rescuer-king'. Jesus draws her attention to his own identity in 4:26:

I who speak to you am he.

He and he alone can give us eternal life and his own life-giving Spirit. His death is the only way back to God, the Father. Trusting Jesus brings life and forgiveness.

Our lives need not remain empty. There is one who will fill us to overflow with forgiveness, love and hope.

With the gift of eternal life.

John 5:1-9

Some time later, Jesus went up to Jerusalem for a feast of the Jews. Now there is in Jerusalem near the Sheep Gate a pool, which in Aramaic is called Bethesda and which is surrounded by five covered colonnades. Here a great number of disabled people used to lie—the blind, the lame, the paralysed. One who was there had been an invalid for thirty-eight years. When Jesus saw him lying there and learned that he had been in this condition for a long time, he asked him, "Do you want to get well?"

"Sir," the invalid replied, "I have no one to help me into the pool when the water is stirred. While I am trying to get in, someone else goes down ahead of me."

Then Jesus said to him, "Get up! Pick up your mat and walk." At once the man was cured; he picked up his mat and walked.

8

About Compassion

A friend of mine was leading a church service in Cape Town when three young men masked with balaclavas burst in, firing guns and throwing hand grenades among the stunned congregation. It was a packed building. There were more than a thousand people. Eleven were murdered. Many were maimed for life.

How can people act like that?

Or consider the terrorist attacks in New York and Washington.

How can people act like that?

Think about the short term and the long-term emotional, as well as physical, impact of these incidents.

How can life become so broken?

So often, with every fibre of our being, we want to cry out, "It's not fair." How can so much suffering come to some people?

Too much suffering for one man
Such questions must leap to mind as we look at the scene described by John in 5:2-3:

> **Now there is in Jerusalem near the sheep gate a pool . . . Here a great number of**

disabled people used to lie—the blind, the lame, the paralysed.

Imagine the stories of suffering that would emerge from this bunch of desperately needy people.

You visit a friend in hospital. You walk past room after room of very ill people. Some long term. Some terminal. Relatives group around beds, pace anxiously in the corridors or step outside for a nervous smoke.

Occasionally you'll make eye contact. Lost eyes. Sad eyes. Eyes full of fear. Eyes without hope. All with a story of suffering and heartache.

What must Jesus have been feeling as he mingled among these blind, lame and paralysed people? This was no modern hospital. The patients weren't in the care of medical staff or in beds with fresh linen. Some would have been abandoned. There was no welfare net. They begged for everything. In 5:5-7 John records:

> **One who was there had been an invalid for thirty-eight years. When Jesus saw him lying there, and learned that he had been in this condition for a long time, he asked him, "Do you want to get well?"**
> **"Sir", the invalid replied, "I have no one to help me into the pool when the water is stirred. While I am trying to get in, someone else goes down ahead of me."**

This man suffered a serious health condition for 38 years. I hate being sick for a day!

That's not the half of it. The man tells Jesus that he has had no one to help him into the pool when the waters were stirred up. The sick probably gathered there because of some superstitious belief that the moving waters had healing power. When the waters were stirred up (we are not told how or why), there was a cut-throat scramble to get into the pool.

Some of the sick had friends or relatives to assist them. But this man didn't—and not being quick enough to heave himself in, he was always too late. Life was the pits for him physically, and to multiply his misery, he was without friends. Life was the pits relationally. He had been hit a double blow.

Life doesn't get much tougher than this.

The source of all sorrow

Why is life so unfair to some? Why is there so much suffering in our world? Why does God allow it to go on?

A common reaction is to blame God for our suffering. The movie *Patch Adams* tells the story of a medical student who uses humour to ease the suffering of his patients. But he is stretched beyond his limits by his girlfriend's brutal murder. On a cliff edge in an isolated forest and tempted to suicide, he argues with God about the issue of suffering:

> You created man. Man suffers enormous amounts of pain. Man dies. You should have had a few more brainstorming sessions prior to creation. You rested the seventh day. Maybe you should have spent that day on compassion.

Rage against the right enemy

This whole issue might be a huge hurdle that stands between you and embracing Christianity. Kids with cancer. Young people with the deep scars of sexual abuse. Generations locked into poverty. Your heart aches. Your brain boils.

I would urge you never to lose your rage against suffering and injustice and evil. But rage against the right enemy. Rage against the devil and sin and evil that is the source of suffering.

Rage against the sin in your own heart!

For suffering is an intruder. An alien. It came with sin. It exists because of our rebellion against God. Jesus hints at this in 5:14. He says to the man he has just healed:

> **See, you are well again. Stop sinning or something worse may happen to you.**

Jesus is not saying that this man was a worse sinner than anyone else or that his 38 years of suffering was a 'singling out' for some sordid past. He gives a clue as to the source of suffering. It is a tragic outcome of our collective rebellion.

Every last one of us has rebelled against God and every single one of us live with the 'scar-marks' of sin in our lives. The details will vary from person to person but the main features remain the same. Suffering and death are the result of sin. To keep rebelling is to invite God's final judgment! To suffer eternal punishment.

The man of compassion

We all hate suffering! But remember that whatever revulsion we feel about it is pale compared to God's hatred of it. How do we know? Really know? Look at Jesus in action.

Jesus knew this man. He knew the Samaritan woman. He knows us. In John 2:25 we read:

> **There was no need for anyone to tell him about them, because he knew what was in their hearts.**

This is awesome stuff. Jesus knows exactly what we are like! He knows our shameful thoughts, deceitful words and concealed motives. He knows our pain, our struggles and our doubts. Talk to him about them. Talk to him about anything. Do you think he's not big enough or understanding enough to handle you? Look at the gentleness he showered on the woman's empty life and the compassion he pours into this man's broken life.

I was fascinated by a report about an Australian Cricket tour to India. On a rare day off in the middle of a long and hard tour, Australia's captain, Steve Waugh, left the air-conditioned comforts of a five star hotel to visit a leprosy orphanage in the poorest area of Calcutta.

There was a pool to relax in. Drinks to order. Emails to check. Team banter to enjoy. Fatigue to overcome. He passed up all that for the squalor of Calcutta! To visit a leprosy orphanage. Would you have done it? Would I?

Jesus could have been content to mix it with Jerusalem's elite. But he preferred the company at the bottom end of town. He could have settled down in the family business, working with his hands and easing into the quiet life most of us dream about for our retirement. He could have remained at his Father's side in the sanity and security of heaven.

Beyond compassion

Where do we find him? Among us. Up to his armpits in the squalor of human suffering. With beggars, sufferers, prostitutes, hypocrites, traitors and rejects. All of life's 'losers'. Not only on a day off. Not only a night of compassion. But for a life mission of love.

God didn't need to spend 'a day' on compassion. It is core to his very being! As one old hymn says, "Jesus, you are all compassion, pure and lavish love you are."

Jesus compassion is not all that shows to this man. With breathtaking simplicity John records in 5:8:

> **Then Jesus said to him, "Get up! Pick up your mat and walk." At once the man was cured; he picked up his mat and walked.**

He heals this poor, friendless, 'legless' man. He mends this broken life. He sets him out on a brand new crack at life. It's like he'd been born all over again. But the big work of healing was still to come.

The sign of something greater

Life is beyond human repair. Some of us will identify with this suffering man. Some with the empty life of the woman who came to a water hole never imagining the crystal clear waterfall she was about to enjoy.

The healing of this broken life points to the great healing that Jesus offers to each of us. In 5:17 Jesus speaks about his and his Father's work:

> **My Father is always at his work to this very day, and I, too, am working.**

Jesus is referring to the man's healing, and on the Sabbath no less! But that greater work of healing is always in view.

When Jesus died on the cross, he paid the penalty that our rebellion deserves. Through Jesus we can be forgiven. We can be restored to that special relationship we were created for. Knowing that when Jesus comes again we can be a part of his perfectly restored universe, living in a perfect relationship with God and his people.

Afraid to hope?

Dying Young is a movie about a young man, dying from

leukaemia, who falls in love with his nurse. In a period of remission they move to a small coastal community.

When his illness returns he tries to hide the painful reality from her and it badly affects their relationship. She discovers the awful truth and pleads to know why he tried to keep her from knowing:

> "Why didn't you tell me?"
> "I was afraid," he responds.

She argues that she was there for him before and would be there again, carrying him to hospital if she had to. Again she pleads to know what he is afraid of. His answer is very telling:

> "I was afraid . . . of hoping."

Have your hopes been smashed by hurt or disappointment one too many times? Don't let that fear keep you from the life Jesus offers. It may sound too good to be true but it just happens to be true.

Jesus, the man of compassion, makes it so.

John 6:25-35

When they found him on the other side of the lake, they asked him, "Rabbi, when did you get here?"

Jesus answered, "I tell you the truth, you are looking for me, not because you saw miraculous signs but because you ate the loaves and had your fill. Do not work for food that spoils, but for food that endures to eternal life, which the Son of Man will give you. On him God the Father has placed his seal of approval."

Then they asked him, "What must we do to do the works God requires?"

Jesus answered, "The work of God is this: to believe in the one he has sent."

So they asked him, "What miraculous sign then will you give that we may see it and believe you? What will you do? Our forefathers ate the manna in the desert; as it is written: 'He gave them bread from heaven to eat.'"

Jesus said to them, "I tell you the truth, it is not Moses who has given you the bread from heaven, but it is my Father who gives you the true bread from heaven. For the bread of God is he who comes down from heaven and gives life to the world."

"Sir," they said, "from now on give us this bread."

Then Jesus declared, "I am the bread of life. He who comes to me will never go hungry, and he who believes in me will never be thirsty."

9

About Satisfaction

Helen and I celebrated a recent anniversary with a big 'cook-up' of each other's favourite food at home.

We shopped separately during the day to keep the courses of this special dinner a surprise. Helen was looking after entree. I was up for the 'mains' and our daughter Kim was taking care of dessert. We had our hunches about the first two courses and were pretty sure dessert would have a chocolate theme to it.

Dinner was fantastic. For the entree, Helen cooked garlic prawns. For the main course I prepared honey glazed barbecue prawns. Dessert was death by chocolate!

There are things that you just can't get enough of. Like seafood and chocolate! While that is a matter of opinion or taste, there are more important things that we crave and hunger for. Like contentment and satisfaction.

But why are most experiences of satisfaction and contentment so short-lived? Why does the hunger return so quickly? Why is lasting satisfaction so elusive?

It shouldn't surprise us that Jesus uses the language of food and drink to tell us that satisfaction in life is found only by trusting him. He says in John 6:35:

I am the bread of life. He who comes to me

will never go hungry and whoever believes in me will never be thirsty.

Universal language

Food is a universal language. All over the world and down through history it has been used to woo lovers and poison kings.

Food replenishes the strength of armies and the tide of war is turned. Company executives are wined and dined, with the billion-dollar deal done on a handshake over cigars and port. Vitamins are measured out with rocket science precision to give elite athletes that millisecond edge.

Jesus uses this universal language as he offers to satisfy our deepest hunger and greatest thirst. These truths of eternity contain both a claim and a promise.

A claim about his credentials and his true identity for he says, **"I am the bread of life."**

A promise about what he can provide for he says, **"He who comes to me will never go hungry."**

His claim

Jesus makes this massive claim after two astonishing events. Firstly, Jesus feeds 5000 people with a couple of tuna sandwiches (John 6:1-15). As a result, this Galilean crowd wants to make him a king. They want Jesus to lead them to drive out their Roman oppressors.

But Jesus retreats to the hills. He will not be party to their political agenda. Meanwhile the disciples attempt a lake crossing in their fishing boat. During the night in a ferocious storm, Jesus comes to them walking on the raging waters. After an initial shock they welcome him aboard and beach on the other side of the lake (6:16-24).

The feeding miracle would have reminded all these Jews, crowd and disciples, of the time their ancestors were sustained by God in the wilderness by the provision of supernatural food (Exodus 16).

Jesus' claim to be the 'bread of life' in the light of this miracle was a way of identifying himself as the God of their fathers. His emphatic 'I AM' reinforces that claim.

He makes the claim that he has already demonstrated in the miracle. The miracle is like a signpost. It points to his real identity. He is a king. But he doesn't have a local political agenda. He is the God and King of the whole universe. The sign also shows us that Jesus loves and cares for his needy people. It assures us of the real hope we can have in him.

The sign of walking on the raging waters reinforces this in another dramatic way. Jesus was effectively showing his disciples that they couldn't manage life without him.

Apart from the Master of wind and waves, our lives are doomed to destruction.

Without the bread of life, spiritual hunger will kill us.

But in relationship with Jesus, submitting to his word, trusting in his rescuing power, we will not perish but have eternal life (John 3:16).

Junk food

When Jesus and the disciples arrive on the other side of the lake, the swelling crowd isn't far behind (6:22-24).

Intrigued as to how Jesus kept a watery step ahead of them, they ask him when he got there (6:25).

Jesus ignores the question and reads their hearts. He says in 6:26-27:

> **I tell you the truth, you are looking for me not because you saw miraculous signs, but because you ate the loaves and had your fill. Do not work for food that spoils, but for food that endures to eternal life, which the Son of Man will give you.**

Firstly, they had tried to take him by force and make him their king. Their minds were filled with politics. Then they chased after him, not because they realised that the sign was to lead them to trust him as their God, but because their physical hunger was satisfied. They were only interested in further material gain. But Jesus shows them that neither material gain nor a political solution is the way to true satisfaction.

Jesus identifies two types of food. One spoils and the other lasts into eternity. Junk food and health food!

Consuming lies

Like these people, and like all people, we never learn. We think that real satisfaction lies in the new, and the next.

A new hobby. The next holiday.

A new outfit. The next car.

A new house. The next partner.

A new career. The next lucky break.

A new government. The next election.

A new season. The next Grand Final.

It never ends. We think we know better but we never wise up.

I find myself smiling in amused agreement with the bumper sticker that says, "I know that money doesn't make you happy, but I'd just like the chance to prove it."

I was walking at the beach and passed an old man with a small child. I guessed they were grandfather and grandson. It was a perfect warm winter's day. The morning sunrays danced on the ocean. He looked at me and said, "This is what life's all about, isn't it." I wanted to agree, but this greater reality that Jesus speaks of made me hesitate.

To take on a half-truth is to take on a lie. Life is more than food and drink, as important as they are. It is more than having good physical health and holidays at the beach. It is more than having the kind of family relationships where you can walk with your grandkids— as attractive and wonderful as they are.

At the heart of life is relationship with Jesus Christ who is our God. We are hungry because that relationship is broken. That hunger will keep tearing at us until the relationship is restored.

His promise

Jesus makes an astounding promise. Hunger will be satisfied. Thirst quenched. How long for? Not for a few hours. Forever. For all eternity. In this life and the next!

It's spiritual language. The promise of a forgiven and restored relationship with the living God. In John chapter 4 he described it as life-giving water. Here he describes it as life-giving bread.

Jesus speaks about working for the right food. He is talking about the true end of their searching. The goal of their labour. But they can think only in terms of working to win God's approval. So they ask in 6:28:

> **What must we do to do the works God requires?**

When it comes to being accepted by God, we always seem to think that it depends on some level of performance. We must reach some standard before God will accept us.

"Have I lived a good enough life? Have I been a good enough person?" We tie ourselves in knots wondering how good is good enough.

Don't you find trying to reach and maintain high performance levels discouraging? I heard that golf sensation Tiger Woods scored his first sub 50 for nine holes of golf at the ripe old age of three! Jack Nicklaus was eight! That's not just discouraging. It's devastating.

At a school I attended, the main hall was full of honour boards and trophy cabinets that made grand statements about achievement and performance and status. All that engraved silverware and polished cedar and gold lettering made mere mortals like me feel that we had nothing at all to contribute.

A friend tells me that there were two honour boards in the main hall at a school he visited in England. On one were the names of past students who were Olympic gold medallists, while the other recorded the names of Nobel Prize winners! Imagine being a struggler at that school.

If acceptance with God were on the basis of some performance criteria where would that leave us? Nobody can ever measure up to God's perfect standard. We are sinful people and every new day gets filled with failures. The record gets stained again and again by our selfish and rebellious thoughts, words and actions.

But the great news is that acceptance with God is not performance-based. It has nothing to do with what I do but on what Jesus has done. The 'work' God requires is not self-reliance but relying on Jesus. Trusting in him for

God's forgiveness and acceptance. Jesus says in 6:29:

The work of God is this: to believe in the one he has sent.

He claims to be our sovereign God. As the sovereign God who knows our hearts, he exposes the folly of our selfish materialism and the futility of our self-reliance.

But he is full of mercy. As our merciful God he shows us that the way to relationship with him depends, not on our work, but trusting in him and his work. This is the way to true satisfaction and only Jesus can nourish us.

This he does with the gift of his own life. The food that endures to eternal life is his life that will be offered up as payment for sins through his death on the cross (6:41-59).

Trusting in Jesus' death brings true satisfaction. A restored relationship with God. The gift of eternal life.

Our hearts will remain hungry until we trust him.

John 8:1-11

Then each went to his own home.

But Jesus went to the Mount of Olives. At dawn he appeared again in the temple courts, where all the people gathered around him, and he sat down to teach them. The teachers of the law and the Pharisees brought in a woman caught in adultery. They made her stand before the group and said to Jesus, "Teacher, this woman was caught in the act of adultery. In the Law Moses commanded us to stone such women. Now what do you say?" They were using this question as a trap, in order to have a basis for accusing him.

But Jesus bent down and started to write on the ground with his finger. When they kept on questioning him, he straightened up and said to them, "If any one of you is without sin, let him be the first to throw a stone at her." Again he stooped down and wrote on the ground.

At this, those who heard began to go away one at a time, the older ones first, until only Jesus was left, with the woman still standing there. Jesus straightened up and asked her, "Woman, where are they? Has no one condemned you?"

"No-one, sir," she said.

"Then neither do I condemn you," Jesus declared. "Go now and leave your life of sin."

10

About Forgiveness

What value do you place on forgiveness? Think of your relationships for a moment. What would they be like without this gift? What are they like when forgiveness has been needed but not asked for? Or has been asked for but not given?

Jesus wants us to make the best discovery we can ever have about life. No matter who we are, what we've done or where we've been, we are not beyond God's forgiveness.

Swimming pool sorrows

When I was the Anglican Minister in a small country town I used to swim at the local indoor heated pool. Late one afternoon, while I was doing some laps, I crashed head on into another swimmer.

Dazed, we both stood up in chest deep water and said some very sharp and unkind things to each other. As quickly as we exchanged these less than pleasant words, we adjusted our goggles (which had been knocked out of place by the collision) and continued our laps.

Swimming along, I started to feel guilty for the way I had spoken to him. Then the thought entered my mind that he might have recognised me and I nearly locked up in fear. So I decided to keep swimming laps until he was gone and on his way home so I'd never have to face him.

I swam about 30 more laps than I'd planned. When he was gone (the pool was now empty as it was nearly closing time) I dragged myself out of the pool exhausted. But I decided to have a quick spa before going home. I dashed over to the spa room and to my horror there was a lone figure in the spa.

I stepped down into the hot bubbly water and we eyed each other off from opposite corners of the spa. He was the first to break the silence and asked:

> "Mate, were you the bloke I ran into in the pool?"
>
> "Yes, I was," I replied.
>
> "Oh mate, I'm really sorry for the way I spoke to you," he said.
>
> "No," I shot back. "I'm the one who should be sorry."
>
> "No mate," he insisted. "I'm the one who should be sorry . . ." We went back and forward like this for a bit and then he added, "I'm the one who's sorry because you don't know what I do for a living."
>
> "What do you do for a living?" I asked.
>
> "I'm a school counsellor. I run special programs in high schools to help kids in trouble with the law to talk sense to themselves and not to lose their temper. The very thing I teach these kids I failed to do. That's why it's me who should be sorry."

We fell back into an awkward silence broken by a bit

of small talk until he asked me the inevitable question:

> "Well mate, what do you do for a living?"
> "I'm the local Anglican Minister here in town. So you can see why it's me who should be sorry."
> "The local Anglican Minister!" he said, stunned. "I lost my temper with a man of the cloth. Oh mate," he said, "I'm doubly sorry!"

We were able to have a good laugh together after that and begin to relate to each other on proper terms. And believe me, it was good to leave the pool that day knowing that he had forgiven me, that the fracture in our relationship had been fixed. To know that when we met in the street we could greet each other openly rather than awkwardly avoiding eye contact.

When you need it, there is nothing like forgiveness. If it is crucial to the health of human relationships, how much more important is it to our relationship with God?

A woman in need

In John 8:1-11 we meet a woman who is brought before Jesus in desperate need. She has been caught in the act of adultery! Was it a keyhole spy job? An unsuspecting husband dropping home for an unexpected surprise? We can only guess how she was 'caught in the act'.

The whole affair is just riddled with rotten motives, blind prejudice and sickening hypocrisy. Where is the slightest regard for human dignity? Where is the male adulterer?

The real reason for the actions of these men comes to light in the question they put to Jesus in 8:4-5:

> **Teacher, this woman was caught in the act of adultery. In the Law, Moses commanded us to stone such women. Now what do you say?**

It was a carefully laid trap and we are told as much in 8:6. Whether the woman is stoned to death or just deeply humiliated is of little concern to her accusers. Her adulterous partner doesn't even enter into the equation. Jesus is the one they have fixed in their sights. He must be neutralised at any cost.

It is a cunning trap. If Jesus lets the woman off, they can accuse him of ignoring the law of Moses. This would justify their opposition to him.

But if he goes with what the law demands and agrees to her being stoned, two things will unravel. He will lose his credibility as a man of mercy and compassion. And he will set himself on a collision course with the Romans who had decreed that they controlled capital punishment.

Jesus sidesteps the trap in breathtaking fashion. He calmly says in 8:7:

> **If anyone of you is without sin, let him be the first to throw a stone at her.**

Caught in a trap tighter than the one they had laid, they drift away, **"from the oldest to the youngest"** (8:9). Jesus' words packed a powerful punch. Every heart was laid bare and everyone's guilt exposed.

Whoever we are

No one is beyond God's forgiveness.

One of the really curious things about life is that there are people who are in no doubt about their need for forgiveness. For many people who meet Jesus, the reality of this forgiveness fills their days with endless wonder and deepest gratitude.

For others, his forgiveness is treated as lightly as if it doesn't matter at all. For many the very idea that they need to be forgiven is offensive to them. Some even think that if there is such a thing as sin and guilt then it must be because God has a hang-up with it.

There's a story about a reluctant teenager who goes to the orthodontist. In trying to build some rapport with his less than cooperative patient, he asks:

> "And what can I do for you, young lady?"
> "Nothin!"
> "Do you have a problem with your teeth?"
> "Nope."
> "Oh, I see. It's not you who has the problem but it's the dentist, your parents and me who have the problem?"
> "Yep."

Sin is our problem and we know it. We all are responsible for the way we've ignored God and we all need God's forgiveness. There's not a single person in history who could have felt secure in the presence of Jesus or stepped up to the stone pit that day.

Wherever we've been
Memory is a powerful thing and sadly for many, if not all of us, there are places we've been, things we've thought and said, hurts we've inflicted, that we wish we could forget but the memory of them won't go away.

In the movie *Sleepers* four youths are sent to a

juvenile justice institution for a reckless prank that resulted in manslaughter. While there, they are subjected to terrible forms of abuse for which they take revenge some time after they are released. Towards the end of the film one of the characters, tired with the memories of a life filled with hatred, abuse and revenge says to one of his friends:

> I just want to close my eyes and not remember
> the places I've been.

There are places we have been, things we have said, hurts we have inflicted. How we wish we could forget them, but their memory returns, accuses and grinds away.

When we really lower our guard and start to be honest with each other, there's not a person amongst us who doesn't secretly long for forgiveness.

Whatever we've done

Like me, you will have met many people who find it very hard to come to terms with things they have done in their lives. They just can't, in their own words, "forgive themselves." I want to take great care here because I am raising a sensitive matter for many troubled people.

I've talked to older men who in their earlier years took human life and inflicted much pain and suffering on others. They have tried to deal with it in their own way but admit that the memory continues to torment them. No amount of reassurance that they were caught up in 'a just war' eases their sense of guilt.

Jealousy and greed may keep siblings from speaking to each other for years or forever.

We may have bought sex, or manipulated it with

words of love, spoken as leverage to satisfy our lust.

There may be deep regrets over the way we have caused hurt to others and caused enormous emotional hardship for them. We may have sought their forgiveness, and received it, but the guilt simmers away.

Condemned by our own conscience, there is a higher court of appeal for such heavy hearts.

The high court of heaven offers this forgiveness.

How can I speak with such confidence? Look at Jesus' words to this frightened and humiliated woman in 8:11:

> **Then neither do I condemn you. Go and leave your life of sin.**

Back in 3:17 John tells us:

> **For God did not send his Son into the world to condemn the world, but to save the world through him.**

Like this woman we are offered, not the punishment we deserve, but the forgiveness that we don't deserve— God's priceless gift of forgiveness.

The price of this gift

This priceless gift has come at a price. What it cost God to purchase our forgiveness is no less than the death of his one and only Son.

The greatest of all gifts comes to us at the greatest of all costs to God.

God's priceless gift of forgiveness.

There is no greater need. There is no greater offer.

Whoever we are. Wherever we've been. Whatever we've done.

John 9:1-11

As he went along, he saw a man blind from birth. His disciples asked him, "Rabbi, who sinned, this man or his parents, that he was born blind?"

"Neither this man nor his parents sinned," said Jesus, "but this happened so that the work of God might be displayed in his life. As long as it is day, we must do the work of him who sent me. Night is coming when no one can work. While I am in the world, I am the light of the world."

Having said this, he spit on the ground, made some mud with the saliva, and put it on the man's eyes. "Go," he told him, "wash in the Pool of Siloam" (this word means Sent). So the man went and washed, and came home seeing.

His neighbors and those who had formerly seen him begging asked, "Isn't this the same man who used to sit and beg?" Some claimed that he was. Others said, "No, he only looks like him."

But he himself insisted, "I am the man."

"How then were your eyes opened?" they demanded.

He replied, "The man they call Jesus made some mud and put it on my eyes. He told me to go to Siloam and wash. So I went and washed, and then I could see."

11

About Blindness

Is it possible to have perfect vision but be blind to the real meaning of life?

Around the time I turned 49, I picked up a newspaper article entitled *Life after 50*. It told me that the first 50 years are about ascent, but after that life is about decline and adjusting to that reality.

I immediately thought of two elderly friends who physically are much frailer than they ever were, but have lived and are living the most productive years of their lives—in their seventies and eighties! Maybe that's why one of them says, "The first 50 years are the hardest!"

How shortsighted, even blind, to see life only in terms of physical age or strength.

There is a powerful image in the Italian movie *Cinema Paradiso*. The old man, Alfredo, the local cinema projector operator, has been totally blinded in an accident. In a later scene, his young protégé, Toto, talks naively about what he wants to do with his life. Blind old Alfredo, concerned for his young friend's future, says, "Right now, you're blinder than I am."

Blinder than the blind

There is a form of blindness that's worse than physical

blindness and there is a form of vision that's better than being able to see. We talk about the value of hindsight and foresight and what we mean is the getting of wisdom.

When it comes to the big issues of life, and the meaning and purpose of life, who has the answers? What is life all about? Who is blind and who can see?

In Chapters 8 and 9 of John's Gospel, John records some remarkable 'footage' from Jesus' life. The two chapters belong together. Jesus uses the language of darkness and light, of blindness and sight, so that we will 'see' the truth that he is our loving Creator who has the right to demand our allegiance and trust. Only in him is there hope of forgiveness and life.

Jesus does this in three ways. In the claim he makes, in the sign he shows and in the sight he gives.

The claim he makes

Jesus makes this claim in 8:12:

> **I am the light of the world. Whoever follows me will never walk in darkness; but will have the light of life.**

In 9:39 he asserts:

> **For judgment I have come into this world, so that the blind will see and those who see will become blind.**

Jesus' focus is both on the here and now and on eternity. He is saying that our experience of true life and our eternal destiny turns on our reception or rejection of him.

The setting for this claim is significant. Jesus is in

Jerusalem at festival time. After the Sydney 2000 Olympics everyone agreed that Australians love to party. Well, the Jews knew how to party also! And not just once every four years. They had several festivals each year, for all the significant events in their history.

This festival was called the *Feast of Tabernacles*. One of its features was the lighting of huge chandeliers in the temple courts. These great torches symbolised the way that God led their ancestors in a pillar of fire, which lit the night sky with an awesome display of light, when he rescued them from Egypt (Exodus 13:17-22).

I am your God

In claiming to be **"the light of the world"**, Jesus is claiming that he is the very God who rescued his people from Egypt. The Jews and their leaders are tuned into this. Throughout the rest of Chapter 8 Jesus is locked in a heavy dispute with them about his claims and his origins and when he declares in 8:58, **"I tell you the truth ... before Abraham was born, I am!"** the claim is beyond doubt.

In declaring, **"I AM!"** Jesus is virtually saying, "I am the God of your great father Abraham. I am the God of your great prophet Moses. I am the God of your great King David!" He is claiming God's name. He is using God's signature.

To the Jewish leaders he has committed the ultimate blasphemy. He has claimed to be God! But as Chapter 9 unfolds Jesus shows that rejection of his claim demonstrates the totality of their spiritual blindness.

Jesus' claim has far reaching implications. He is our God and is worthy of our worship. Without him we are blind and our lives are in darkness.

We Australians like to see ourselves as successful and clever so it's hard for us to believe that. We may be good at sport, but do we really have life together? Our divorce rate and youth suicide rate are among the highest in the world. We are failing at relationships and failing our kids, but we claim to be clever and 'enlightened'.

We are like this because we have failed at the most important relationship of all. The relationship God created for us to enjoy with him. Having broken that relationship it follows that we would have a pretty poor track record in the other relationships that God gave us to enjoy in his world.

That's the darkness Jesus is referring to. It's spiritual and moral. The Bible uses language like blindness and death to describe the reality and seriousness of it.

We are in darkness. We are blind. We have pushed God to the edge of our existence. We've assigned our Creator to a cameo role. We have relegated the captain to the bench. We have pushed the conductor into the choir.

It's bizarre behaviour. It attracts his judgment and deserves the punishment of hell. The darkness is real and frightening.

The sign he shows

The whole purpose of Jesus' coming among us is to break the power of this darkness. How can we be sure that Jesus can deliver what he promises? In Chapter 9 he heals a man who has been blind from birth. Jesus miraculously heals this blind beggar. He claims to be the light of the world. He proves that he has the power to conquer the darkness in this amazing action.

The healing is recorded with stunning simplicity.

After a discussion with the disciples about the reason for the man being born blind, Jesus claims once again to be **"the light of the world."** John then describes what follows (9:6-7):

> **Having said this, he spit on the ground, made some mud with the saliva and put it on the man's eyes. "Go," he told him, "wash in the pool of Siloam." (This word means Sent). So the man went and washed, and came home seeing.**

The miracle itself is astonishing. But here comes the real shock. If the miracle is unexpected (as all miracles are by nature) what follows is unexpected in the extreme.

The chapter begins with a man in total darkness. It ends with religious people in total darkness and the once blind beggar having both physical and spiritual sight. A man blind from birth can see in every way while 'religious experts' are judged by Jesus to be totally blind.

Shades of darkness

This is reinforced as John records five conversations.

Firstly, between the blind man and his neighbours in 9:8-12. Some of them refuse to believe that the man standing before them with 20/20 vision is the same man they knew to be blind from birth. Despite the evidence they continue to disbelieve. They are blind.

Secondly, we are shown the 'blindness' of the man's parents in 9:18-23. The Jewish leaders had decided to ban from the synagogue anyone who acknowledged Jesus to be 'the Christ'. The parents fail to stand by their own son for fear of rejection. They too are blind.

Thirdly, John records a series of sharp dialogues between the healed man and the Jewish leaders (9:13-17; 9:24-34). They interrogate him as to his view about Jesus' identity. They are more concerned that the miracle took place on their 'day of rest' than about rejoicing in the man's sight. More blindness!

The healed man is unshaken by their threats of expulsion and answers their questions with honesty and courage (9:17; 9:24-27; 9:30-33). The man's pluck serves to highlight the theme of darkness/light and blindness/sight that's weaving its way through the whole gripping episode. There is much blindness all around this now seeing—and insightful—man.

But it is the 'spiritual sight' that Jesus gives that really floods hope into human life.

The sight he gives

We are told in 9:34 that the Jewish leaders throw the healed man out of the synagogue. It is a dark moment in Jewish history. But John records the fourth conversation and Jesus' actions in 9:35:

> **Jesus heard that they had thrown him out, and when he found him, he said, "Do you believe in the Son of Man?"**

Jesus hears of the man's plight, looks for and finds him. It's like the language that Jesus uses when speaking about a shepherd who leaves ninety-nine sheep in safety to search for the one that is lost. In the very next chapter of John's Gospel Jesus will identify himself as the 'good shepherd' who lays down his life for the sheep.

What a contrast! These false shepherds cold-heartedly

banish the man from the synagogue. Jesus is the true shepherd who goes in search of this lost 'spiritually blind' person and every lost and spiritually blind person. He has come in search of us. Like the true and good shepherd who lays down his life for the sheep, we can be sure that through his death for us, our spiritual blindness can be healed. Our way back to God has been secured.

This is the sight he gives.

Believing is seeing

The man responds to Jesus. In 9:38 John records:

> **Then the man said, "Lord I believe", and he worshiped him.**

To worship Jesus means to obey him. To follow Jesus means to trust him. To relate to Jesus with trust, obedience and worship is what spiritual sight is about.

The Jewish leaders who refuse to do this prove their own spiritual blindness. Those who come to Jesus admitting their prior blindness, receive his gift of spiritual sight. (The fifth conversation is in 9:39-41.)

An elderly friend of mine was waiting for risky and delicate surgery on her rapidly failing eyesight. I asked her if she was afraid of the operation. Her reply was honest. "Yes", she said, "but you don't say 'no' to sight".

Will you say "yes" or "no" to sight?

John 10:7-18

Therefore Jesus said again, "I tell you the truth, I am the gate for the sheep. All who ever came before me were thieves and robbers, but the sheep did not listen to them.

"I am the gate; whoever enters through me will be saved. He will come in and go out, and find pasture. The thief comes only to steal and kill and destroy; I have come that they may have life, and have it to the full.

"I am the good shepherd. The good shepherd lays down his life for the sheep. The hired hand is not the shepherd who owns the sheep. So when he sees the wolf coming, he abandons the sheep and runs away. Then the wolf attacks the flock and scatters it. The man runs away because he is a hired hand and cares nothing for the sheep.

"I am the good shepherd; I know my sheep and my sheep know me—just as the Father knows me and I know the Father—and I lay down my life for the sheep. I have other sheep that are not of this sheep pen. I must bring them also. They too will listen to my voice, and there shall be one flock and one shepherd. The reason my Father loves me is that I lay down my life—only to take it up again. No one takes it from me, but I lay it down of my own accord. I have authority to lay it down and authority to take it up again. This command I received from my Father."

12

About Security

We have a children's picture book at home called *Would You Rather*? When our kids were young it was a family favourite. Each double page has a number of teasing choices about scary, but exaggerated situations in life. One page asks:

> Would you rather be crushed by a huge snake,
> eaten by a crocodile, swallowed by a whale or
> sat on by a rhinoceros?

Each of these scenes is presented with big graphic colour pictures. We would have hot debates about which choice would result in the least pain.

Another that generated fun and fierce debate was:

> Would you rather your Mum had an argument
> in a shop (while you were there), or your Dad
> did a dance in front of your school class?

Whatever the set of choices the book put before us, we argued endlessly for what we thought would involve the least pain or mildest embarrassment.

I have rarely met a person who doesn't need to feel and be safe. What parent doesn't have this concern for their kids foremost in his or her mind?

We take all sorts of measures to ensure our safety and security in this life. Do we apply the same care to the next life and where we will spend eternity?

The care Jesus takes

Concern for our eternal welfare is something Jesus takes very seriously. Think about the wonder of his commitment to our welfare as we look at John Chapter 10.

The picture language Jesus uses may seem a little unusual to urban dwellers—strange even to present day sheep graziers! Jesus' words plunge us into the first century world of sheep farming where flocks were almost like family and shepherds almost like parents. There was the constant threat of predators, danger and death and the need for provision, protection and safety.

Sheep were known and called by name. They knew their shepherd's voice. He would lead them by walking ahead and they would follow. It was that personal and it is still like that in the Middle East today.

Jesus' claim to be **"the good shepherd"** (yet another way of claiming to be our God) shows us that he is the God who provides for and protects his people.

Absolute security

Jesus is promising a life of absolute security. He lays his life on the line for it. He says in 10:11-12:

> **I am the good shepherd. The good shepherd lays down his life for the sheep. The hired hand is not the shepherd who owns the sheep. So when he sees the wolf coming, he abandons the sheep and runs away.**

The contrast here is between the cowardice of an uncaring hired hand and the faithfulness of the flock's true owner. Jesus has the shameful behaviour of the religious leaders in his sights (John 9).

By contrast Jesus is like a true shepherd who will protect his people with his own life (10:11-12). He will also give true and loving leadership to his people (10:3). He will rescue and provide for his people (10:9).

This promise points to Jesus' own death. There he secures his people's eternal safety from God's judgment by paying the penalty for sin.

The promise of absolute security does not mean that people who belong to Jesus walk through this life with 'bullet-proof' protection. They may get cancer, have car accidents, travel in hijacked aircraft and work and worship in buildings that get attacked by terrorists.

Absolute security is eternal security. In the midst of the very uncertainties that surround and threaten our lives, it means that nothing can destroy the security we have in Jesus. Nothing can separate us from his love.

The security industry
Security is a global growth industry. I have a friend in Johannesburg who lives in a two-storey house that is secured by iron bars and high fences. They even have a heavy iron gate in the stairway leading to the upstairs bedrooms. As an extra line of defence, they lock it on their way to bed each night!

In another city in South Africa I heard that a high security fence was erected around a church property. A short time later the security fence was stolen!

How we long for real security! But I'm not just talking about protecting property. People are infinitely more valuable than property. We ache for the welfare of people and especially the people we love.

I will never forget a sunny winter afternoon on the South Coast several years ago. I stood in a fish co-op cold room holding on to a man my own age as he identified the bodies of five family members. They had been washed into the sea from a rock platform where, only hours earlier, they were enjoying a family outing.

In that makeshift morgue, I realised that life is short, uncertain, and insecure. We live constantly in the threatening shadow of death. Is there any hope for eternal security? Jesus points us to himself. To heed his voice. To follow him.

How we need this security. Where have we been led by following any voice other than our God's? Where have the smooth and seductive voices of consumerism and popular culture led us?

Purpose eludes us. Bondage to the 'what's in this for me?' mentality spoils us, shames us and wrecks our relationships. Emptiness engulfs us and death robs us of everything that's worth staying alive for.

Do you think I'm exaggerating? Steve Biddulph, on the subject of men's issues has written in his book *Manhood* (1995) of Australian men:

> Our marriages fail. Our kids hate us. We die from stress and along the way we destroy the world.

Does that sound like our most valuable assets are safe and sound?

Jesus, the good shepherd speaks. Don't ignore his voice. Only he can give us true, eternal security.

Intimate friendship

Jesus' promise of absolute security is also a unique promise of friendship. He adds in 10:14-15:

> **I am the good shepherd. I know my sheep and my sheep know me—just as the Father knows me and I know the Father . . .**

This is an astonishing promise. On offer is a relationship of such closeness and intimacy that when Jesus tries to describe it, he compares it to the relationship that God the Father, and God the Son, have shared for all eternity.

Our God, in the very essence of his Being, is a God in relationship; three persons in perfect harmony—Father, Son and Spirit. We were created to be in relationship with this God. Friendship is at the heart of Christianity.

Surprised by friendship

Sometimes friendship is found in the most unlikely places. At the 1994 Australian Tennis Open, Pete Sampras and Jim Courier were playing in a quarter final. Sampras' coach, Tom Gullikson, had collapsed the day before and lay very ill in a nearby Melbourne hospital.

Sampras was playing well below his best and someone in the crowd yelled out, "Do it for your coach." This made Sampras visibly upset. Heard only by a few courtside media officials and picked up by the TV microphones, Jim whispered over the net, "We don't have to do this, Pete."

In the midst of an elite sporting contest, friendship was the real winner.

Could there be a more surprising place to discover

friendship than in the outstretched hand of friendship that Jesus offers to each of us?

I'm not talking about the friendship of equals. He will always be our God and King and is to be honoured in that way. But it is real friendship and there is only one friendship in the universe like it!

Unconditional forgiveness

How is it possible to be sure of this security, to receive such friendship with God? For although we were created for it, we have forfeited it. We have ignored his voice.

We need forgiveness.

Jesus is like a good shepherd who instinctively lays down his life for the sheep (10:11 and 15). He is like a warrior who defends to the death. A king who goes into battle for his people. But the language quickly moves from picture to reality in verses 17 and 18:

> **The reason my Father loves me is that I lay down my life . . . No one takes it from me, but I lay it down of my own accord.**

When he was two years old we lost our son while picnicking with a few families. He disappeared while we were getting the fire ready for a BBQ. Below us was a river. Above us, an outcrop of rocky ledges and beyond us, thick, untracked forest.

What were we to do? Search on an empty stomach or enjoy the BBQ first? Cool off in the river and see if he wandered back? Our child was lost! Hunger and heat no longer mattered. Only one thing mattered . . .

We spread out in every direction and twenty minutes later I saw him along a trail near the riverbank. I called out to him. He heard my voice and turned and we ran to each other. You will know what I mean when I tell you that gathering him up into my arms that day was one of the most joyful moments of my life.

The shepherd language both here and in so many other places in the Bible brings into sharp focus God's love for his lost people and the great rescue mission of Jesus, the good shepherd.

How does he rescue? He does what a true shepherd does. He puts his body between those he loves and the danger they face. He lays down his life.

Jesus speaks of his approaching death. This is the specific purpose for Jesus' coming into the world. There he would take the full measure of the punishment our rebellion deserved. There he would make forgiveness a reality.

Unconditional forgiveness.

Intimate friendship.

Absolute security.

For those who respond to his voice and follow him.

John 11:17-27

On his arrival, Jesus found that Lazarus had already been in the tomb for four days. Bethany was less than two miles from Jerusalem, and many Jews had come to Martha and Mary to comfort them in the loss of their brother.

When Martha heard that Jesus was coming, she went out to meet him, but Mary stayed at home.

"Lord," Martha said to Jesus, "if you had been here, my brother would not have died. But I know that even now God will give you whatever you ask."

Jesus said to her, "Your brother will rise again."

Martha answered, "I know he will rise again in the resurrection at the last day."

Jesus said to her, "I am the resurrection and the life. He who believes in me will live, even though he dies; and whoever lives and believes in me will never die. Do you believe this?"

"Yes, Lord," she told him, "I believe that you are the Christ, the Son of God, who was to come into the world."

13

About Hope

I was watching a professional golf tournament on TV. At one of the Par 3 holes a very unusual prize was being offered for a 'hole in one' by one of the tournament sponsors.

The sponsor was a funeral company. The prize was a free funeral or a cash payout less than the value of the funeral. The advertising board behind the tee was emblazoned with the slogan: *The Money or the Box.*

I watched with interest to see whether anyone 'aced' the hole and the choice they would make. It didn't happen. But my guess was, although the funeral was a better financial option, the winner would have taken the cash.

We can joke and laugh at death from a safe distance, but that is just where we like to keep it. But never to face its certainty and our own mortality is to deny reality.

Serious joking about death
Some clever lines about death highlight our common fear. One of the most famous is Woody Allen's, "It's not that I'm afraid to die. I just don't want to be there when it happens." That makes another by Allen all the more fascinating, "I don't want to achieve immortality by

being famous. I just want to achieve it by staying alive."

On his deathbed Oscar Wilde said, "This wallpaper is appalling. One of us will have to go." A very famous quote goes like this, "Die! Die! that's the last thing I'll do." Another comes from Joseph Heller who wrote *Catch 22*, "I've decided to live forever or die in the attempt."

A death line with a difference

There is no attempt at funny 'one-liners' by Jesus when it comes to death. Death was no laughing matter for the Creator of life. When it comes to this old enemy, what Jesus refuses to humour, he more than makes up for with his offer of hope. In John 11:25 and 26 he claims:

I am the resurrection and the life. Whoever believes in me will live, even though he dies, and whoever lives and believes in me will never die.

Jesus has already made some astonishing claims. He claimed to be to life what bread is to daily energy (John 6) and what water is to our daily survival (John 4 and 7). He claimed to be light to a traveller in darkness (John 8) and a shepherd to endangered sheep (John 10).

If we don't have food and water, we die. If we don't have light, there's a good chance we'll get mugged and left for dead. If we're a sheep and we don't have a good shepherd, we'll more than likely stumble over a cliff or wander into the jaws of a dingo . . . we're as good as dead.

If we don't have Jesus, we're . . .

Now someone is dead. Dead for four days. Can the one who has given to the lame their legs back and to the blind their sight back; can he, will he give life to this corpse?

A friend is dead

John begins this amazing chapter in Jesus' life (and no less amazing chapter in Lazarus' life) by telling us that Lazarus was sick (11:1). By the time Jesus gets to the village Lazarus has been dead for four days (11:17).

We also learn that Jesus loved Lazarus and his sisters, Mary and Martha, with deep affection (11:3 and 5).

When Jesus finally arrives Martha appears to be angry that Jesus has got there too late to heal Lazarus' sickness, but is confident that Jesus can at least appeal to God for his help. She believed in the common hope that there would be a great resurrection at the end of time (11:24). But she had no inkling of the scope of the miracle that was about to impact her life that day.

Saying the right thing to someone who is grieving is always a delicate matter. I grope around to find a simple expression of comfort that is anchored in the truth, and genuinely seeks to ease the pain.

In the tragic face of death we need words that are true and comforting. Empty sentiment is ultimately neither loving nor helpful. We need words that are true.

Put yourself in Martha's sandals and imagine how she felt when Jesus states:

Your brother will rise again (11:23).
I am the resurrection and the life (11:25).

What a claim Jesus makes to Martha! She is in deep grief and probably still in shock. However well meant, if these words are not true, they are among the most callous ever uttered.

But if they are true? Entertain the thought for a moment that Jesus' promise is true. What difference would that make to life? How would reality be reshaped?

The power of death

I was twelve years old when I first saw a dead body. My sister and I were walking along an isolated beach. An old fisherman warned us not to keep walking in that direction because a man had been washed out to sea and the police had been notified.

We were intrigued and kept walking. When the body washed back to shore and I saw the drowned man close up, it was like I'd smashed into a brick wall. I was deeply affected and shocked. Death was horrible beyond my imagination. I couldn't sleep for nights.

When, as an adult, I have been in the presence of a corpse, my reaction has been just as strong. Death! So final. So powerful. So wrong.

I've already mentioned the day I tried to comfort a man while he identified five members of his family who were washed off a rock platform by a freak wave.

I held this broken man while he gently caressed and kissed the lifeless bodies of his wife, son and sister. How I longed to pull out a bottle of life-fixing medicine, say some commanding words or massage an area of skin and muscle, and see life surge back where death now reigned.

We are powerless before this awesome enemy.

Jesus claims otherwise. In the face of a person's death and its impact on the lives of loved ones and a whole community, how does Jesus react? In 11:33-36 we read:

When Jesus saw (Mary) weeping and the

**Jews who had come along with her also
weeping, he was deeply moved in spirit and
troubled. "Where have you laid him?" he
asked.**
"Come and see, Lord," they replied.
Jesus wept.
Then the Jews said, "See how he loved him!"

Jesus is 'deeply moved'. In the face of death and the
heartbreak it brings to grieving loved ones, Jesus is
enraged. He is angry to the very core of his being.

Have you ever been in a situation where someone you
love has been hurt or their life has been put at risk by an
act of evil or negligence? Everything inside you shakes.
Your guts churn. Your whole being groans for the hurt to
stop and the wrong to be righted.

I was called to a local hospital to visit a small boy one
night. A drunk driver mounted the footpath where he
was playing and ran him down. His brain injuries were
massive. When I saw him my body shook with rage.

This is the force of Jesus' reaction. He hates death. He
hates death with a passion. He hates its menacing threat.
Its life-stealing existence. Don't think God hates death
any less than you. Any way you rage against it would
look like apathy next to his white-hot hatred for it.

Jesus hates death because he loves life. He hates the
reason death has invaded our lives. He is the
compassionate God who hates the misery that death
brings to the creation he loves. To the people he loves.

God in tears
The other emotion that John records is that Jesus weeps
(11:35). Tears of compassion flow freely down the
sunbaked cheeks of God. The obscenity of death is the

111

mockery it makes of life. The mockery it makes of the Creator of life. The pain it brings to friends, families and communities. The pain it brings to the heart of God.

When life meets death, would you expect anything less than these reactions from life's author? Would you expect anything less than a hostile encounter?

They take Jesus to a cave entry covered by a large stone (11:38). Jesus asks for the stone to be removed (11:39). Martha protests. The events of the last days had taken a huge toll without the trauma of her brother's corpse being exhumed and the horrid smell of rotting flesh. But Jesus appeals for her trust.

Words echo inside the cave: **"Lazarus, come out!"** (11:43) Four days dead and Jesus calls the corpse to life. Decomposing flesh, but he doesn't flinch.

John simply says, **"The dead man came out."** (11:44)

Who is this Jesus?

Jesus confirms his claim and keeps his promise. He is the bread of life, the light of the world, the good shepherd.

He is the resurrection and the life.

The Creator of life here recreates. He is our Sovereign God who confronts the savage impact of death on human life. Death does not prevail. Life himself conquers.

Don't miss what Jesus wants us to get. In 11:4 and in 11:40 Jesus speaks of seeing the glory of God. This theme first appears in 1:14 and returns again and again throughout the Gospel. It is reaching its climax. Exactly who God is and what he is like; the power God has and how much he cares for us is seen in the person of Jesus. It is a perfect 'like Father, like Son' thing.

The miraculous signs throughout John's Gospel

showed the disciples the 'glory of Jesus'. From the water changed into wine to this buried body brought back to life, the disciples were 'spellbound' or 'gobsmacked' by what they saw (1:14).

In the person of Jesus, God was in their presence.

The question of trust

This episode brings into view that simple definition of Christianity. It is all about Jesus. It is all about life. It is all about trust. Get that and you've got it.

Jesus is moving Martha beyond facts and into a personal response. Jesus asked Martha in 11:26 if she trusted him. Martha answers the question, but it hangs in the air. Jesus, who has conquered death, calls for our trust.

But reactions to Jesus are divided. Some people place their trust in him (11:45). Others are unmoved and, if anything, are more determined to have Jesus eliminated to protect their own interests (11:46-48).

Death threatens. My death. Your death. But in the one who claims, promises and proves to be the giver of resurrection life, there is genuine hope.

A hope that will be made possible through his own death and resurrection.

PART THREE

A DEATH ABOUT LIFE

The following chapters take us to the events surrounding Jesus' death, resurrection and resurrection sightings.

We will start at Chapter 12 of John's Gospel and then jump to Chapters 18 to 20 of the Gospel.

Chapters 13 to 17 of John's Gospel deal with the events on the night before Jesus trial and execution. I plan to deal with this section of the Gospel in another book.

We come to the very heart of Christianity.

John 12:20-33

Now there were some Greeks among those who went up to worship at the Feast. They came to Philip, who was from Bethsaida in Galilee, with a request. "Sir," they said, "we would like to see Jesus." Philip went to tell Andrew; Andrew and Philip in turn told Jesus.

Jesus replied, "The hour has come for the Son of Man to be glorified. I tell you the truth, unless a kernel of wheat falls to the ground and dies, it remains only a single seed. But if it dies, it produces many seeds. The man who loves his life will lose it, while the man who hates his life in this world will keep it for eternal life. Whoever serves me must follow me; and where I am, my servant also will be. My Father will honour the one who serves me.

"Now my heart is troubled, and what shall I say? 'Father, save me from this hour'? No, it was for this very reason I came to this hour. Father, glorify your name!"

Then a voice came from heaven, "I have glorified it, and will glorify it again." The crowd that was there and heard it said it had thundered; others said an angel had spoken to him.

Jesus said, "This voice was for your benefit, not mine. Now is the time for judgment on this world; now the prince of this world will be driven out. But I, when I am lifted up from the earth, will draw all men to myself." He said this to show the kind of death he was going to die.

14

About Jesus' Death

I've been to some strange dinner parties in my time. Some were unusual because of the wacky things that happened. Others because of the people who were there.

I was at a dinner where the hostess wished to show off the dinner set she had just bought. To demonstrate its unbreakable qualities she threw a plate onto the polished floorboards of the dining room. You guessed it. The plate smashed into a dozen jagged pieces. It was an unforgettable night.

One celebrity I read about said that the guest list at his ideal dinner party would include William Shakespeare, Sir Donald Bradman and Jesus of Nazareth.

Who would you invite to your ideal party?

The party that has it all

In Chapter 12:1-2 John describes a dinner party:

> **Six days before the Passover, Jesus arrived at Bethany where Lazarus lived, whom Jesus had raised from the dead. Here a dinner was given in Jesus' honour. Martha served, while Lazarus was among those reclining at the table with him.**

This party had the lot! Memorable guests. An unforgettable moment. Think of the guests for starters. John mentions four by name. Lazarus, the man Jesus had just raised from the dead. Mary and Martha who were Lazarus' sisters. Martha was helping to serve the food while Mary had a plan, as we shall see. Jesus we are told was the guest of honour.

Imagine eating at the same table with a man who had been dead for four days. Rubbing shoulders with him would have made your hair dance on the back of your neck. Jesus, the man who brought Lazarus back to life, is there too! Washing down his food with some of the best local wine, sharing a joke and chatting with the guests.

Now think about the unusual thing that happens while the party is in full swing. In 12:3 John records:

Then Mary took about half a litre of pure nard, an expensive perfume; she poured it on Jesus' feet and wiped his feet with her hair. And the house was filled with the fragrance of the perfume.

It was quite an attention grabber, bringing the table talk to a grinding halt. But it divided the guests. What follows (12:4-8) is a sharp exchange of words between Judas, the disciple who would betray Jesus, and Jesus himself.

Judas objects. He criticises Mary for her extravagance. Jesus quickly defends her by saying to Judas (12:7):

Leave her alone . . . It was intended that she should save this perfume for the day of my burial.

Death is in the air

Mary's action is an act of lavish love and appreciation to Jesus for Lazarus' life. But it's the spin Jesus puts on it that would have lifted this dinner party to another level.

Jesus is saying that her actions are a kind of advanced 'sign' of his approaching death—a preview of the anointing of his body for burial that Joseph and Nicodemus will soon undertake (19:38-42). The sweet smell of perfume wafting through the air is signalling to every dinner guest that the guest of honour, who has just brought a man back to life, is now preparing for his own death!

What do you talk about after that? A friend of mine says that if you want to bring a dinner conversation to a swift end, lean over and ask your host in a staged whisper; "Have you thought about your death lately?"

Jesus has brought the subject of his own death to the table in a way that would have grabbed everyone's attention!

Death is everywhere

This is a significant turning point in the Gospel. The focus now falls sharply on Jesus' death. It has been in the background throughout the Gospel, but in Chapters 11 and 12 the mood and the pace change rapidly.

Jesus' enemies are committed to planning his betrayal and death (11:45-57). Jesus is painfully aware of the 'hour' of his suffering and death (12:20-36). He knew that his **"time"** (2:4 and 13:1) and **"hour"** (12:23 and 27) were close. The time and hour for which he was born—to die!

The flow of these two chapters is also startling. Chapter 11 begins with Jesus raising Lazarus from the dead. A sign that confirmed Jesus' claim to be **"the resurrection and the life."** It ends with a ruthless plan to take Jesus' life.

Chapter 12 begins with a dinner in honour of Jesus. He has just given life to another. It ends with Jesus making a prediction about the certainty and closeness of his own death—a death that would give life to many others. In the midst of life, the aroma of death hangs in the air.

In Chapter 12:20-36 Jesus speaks about what his death will achieve. This is triggered by a bunch of Greeks who are in Jerusalem and would like to meet Jesus (12:20-22). The fact that some people who are not Jews show interest in Jesus is a sign that Jesus' death is for the whole world, for both the Jewish and non-Jewish world. Jesus responds (12:23-24) by saying:

> **The hour has come for the Son of Man to be glorified. I tell you the truth, unless a kernel of wheat falls to the ground and dies, it remains a single seed. But if it dies it produces many seeds.**

There's that word glory again! It is linked to his death. It will be in his death that the greatest moment of glory arrives. His death will be the supreme public display of God's character. In 12:31-33 we read:

> **"Now is the time for judgment on this world; now the prince of this world will be driven out. But I, when I am lifted up from the earth will draw all men to myself." He said this to show the kind of death he was going to die.**

Jesus says that three things will happen when he dies. The world is judged. The 'prince of this world' is driven out. The people of the world are drawn to him.

Jesus' death and the world's judgment

Judgment is an unpopular idea. But you can't read the Gospel and escape it. Nor can you come to grips with Christianity by ignoring it. Jesus speaks about it throughout the Gospel. In 3:18 he says:

> **Whoever does not believe stands condemned already, because he has not believed in the name of God's one and only Son.**

How does judgment work in the Gospel? Jesus took the judgment we deserve so we could receive the forgiveness we don't deserve. We will not be condemned, but forgiven, if we place our trust in Jesus. We will be condemned, and not forgiven, if we don't place our trust in Jesus.

Plain for all to see

Back in the 1970s I celebrated the end of my exams at an agricultural college by hitchhiking to Queensland to visit a friend. On one of these trips I was given a ride by a couple of 'hotheads' in an old Holden station wagon.

On a mountain pass we were caught behind a semi-trailer on a steep part of the highway. Taking a huge risk the driver swerved out over the double lines and illegally passed the large 'rig'. At the top of the mountain we were pulled over by a policeman. The driver was in disbelief, wondering how his illegal overtake was detected back down the mountain.

As we were motioned out of the car the driver started

to rehearse all kinds of excuses against being charged.

"I'll say the truck had stopped or that it was rolling back and I had no choice but to pass to get out of the road," I heard him muttering to his mate.

When the policeman informed the driver of his driving offence, out trotted the limp excuses. So the policeman quietly asked them to follow him over to the edge of the mountain top. I followed.

Without a word he pointed down to the part of the highway where the offence occurred. It was in full view to all of us. It was amazing how the excuses just dried up. The policeman didn't have to say a word. The driver's guilt was plain for all to see.

When we stand before God on the day of judgment, we will know whether or not Jesus and his death have been the greatest and most valued realities in our life. Mouths will fall open. We will fall silent. Excuses will dry up. There will be pardon for those who have put their trust in Jesus and his death. There will be the punishment of hell for those who have not.

Jesus' death and Satan's downfall

Jesus speaks of driving out the prince of this world. It is Jesus' title for Satan. It is a timely reminder that the world God made through his Son (1:1), and the world God loves and came to rescue through his Son (3:16), is ruled by an evil prince. For the rescue to be achieved, a battle must be fought. An enemy must be overthrown.

It would be a fair thing to ask whether Jesus has really got it right. What does it mean when he speaks of his death producing victory over his enemy, the Devil?

It hardly makes sense. Could he just be riding on a wave of confidence? After all he has just called a man back from the grave. He continues to evade the net that the Jews are tightening around him. His Father's voice has just thundered from heaven saying that his moment of greatest glory is about to arrive.

But how can there be glory in his death? Death by crucifixion? Days later he will hang on a roughly made timber frame, with thrashed flesh tearing away from his body.

Hardly a scene that suggests he is God who has the upper hand in battle, let alone delivering the decisive blow. But that is Jesus' claim. In the next chapter we will see how it works.

Jesus' death and his people rescued

The third thing that Jesus says will happen at his death is that he **"will draw all men"** (12:32) to himself. These words take us back to the earlier moment when a few Greeks asked to see Jesus. In this request, Jesus sees a fulfillment of time and promise.

Jesus' great rescuing work was not restricted to one nation or gender or generation or social class. The **"all men"** he refers to means people of every nation. His rescue is for all humanity.

The death of Jesus. Who would have thought that so much could hang on that black Friday so long ago?

The world's judgment.

Evil's overthrow.

People drawn back to God . . .

John 19:23-30

When the soldiers crucified Jesus, they took his clothes, dividing them into four shares, one for each of them, with the undergarment remaining. This garment was seamless, woven in one piece from top to bottom.

"Let's not tear it," they said to one another. "Let's decide by lot who will get it."

This happened that the scripture might be fulfilled which said,

> "They divided my garments among them and
> cast lots for my clothing."

So this is what the soldiers did.

Near the cross of Jesus stood his mother, his mother's sister, Mary the wife of Clopas, and Mary Magdalene. When Jesus saw his mother there, and the disciple whom he loved standing nearby, he said to his mother, "Dear woman, here is your son," and to the disciple, "Here is your mother." From that time on, this disciple took her into his home.

Later, knowing that all was now completed, and so that the Scripture would be fulfilled, Jesus said, "I am thirsty." A jar of wine-vinegar was there, so they soaked a sponge in it, put the sponge on a stalk of the hyssop plant, and lifted it to Jesus' lips. When he had received the drink, Jesus said, "It is finished." With that, he bowed his head and gave up his spirit.

15

More About Jesus' Death

In a quiet valley in the mountain range behind Sydney, I joined in a memorial service in a small village graveyard. One of the locals spoke about the man who had died. He concluded by saying, "Our friend was a good bloke and he died the way he wanted to; with his boots on."

It is a good description of the way we Australians think about how life should be lived. Especially Australian men. Be a good bloke. Be a hard worker.

Don't get me wrong. They are good qualities. But I have a fear that we think these qualities are the ones that will win God's acceptance and a place in heaven.

Being on top

Our national identity has been hammered out in the face of winning over adversity.

In the twentieth century alone there were two world wars and a great depression from which we emerged stronger and more resilient to rebuild from the ruins.

Through dramatic changes in our ethnic mix, we Australians have discovered a growing maturity in our cultural diversity and tolerance. We are a nation overflowing with newfound confidence.

Never is our self-confidence more evident than when we play sport. We love to beat the English at cricket, the All Blacks (New Zealand) at rugby and the South Africans at both. We really love to beat anybody at anything. We entered a new century at the top of the heap in more sports than seems possible for our population. Then came the Sydney Olympics!

But how foolish to let this kind of self-confidence spill over into our thinking about how we relate to God.

Also, what is it about us that we find it so hard to ask for and receive the help of others? Or when we do receive help, to feel that we must pay it back rather than to accept it as a gift?

This deep-rooted self-reliance is not just a product of a growing national identity. The Bible says it lies deep in the heart of every human being.

The heart of the problem

The Bible says the heart of the problem is our rejection of God. Although created by God to live a life of obedience and trust towards him, we have dragged our feet or dug in our heels altogether. We want to live our own way, not his. And foolishly, we think we can get away with it.

But we are all guilty before God. We are in desperate need of help. We need to be forgiven by our Creator.

Jesus died to rescue us. In John 19:30 we read:

Jesus said, "It is finished."

These are not words of resignation or defeat, but a cry to mark a great victory. Jesus has accomplished what he set out to do. He has done what we could not do. He has done what we can't even lend assistance in doing.

On that 'good' Friday, Jesus' shout of victory declares that he has paid in full the penalty for our rebellion against God. His very death declares the seriousness of sin, and his victorious defeat of sin and death.

Sin is a serious problem

As an Australian I'm part of a culture that takes a lot of serious things lightly. Something is wrong only if you get caught and if you can't scam your way out of it!

But we know that acting selfishly and abusing the law has a disastrous impact on people's value and welfare. It says that people don't matter. It says that a person's integrity isn't worth protecting.

Imagine what would happen if word got around that police had stopped enforcing road rules altogether. How long before it would be too dangerous to venture out as a driver, or even as a pedestrian? Police enforce the law because we live in a society that values life.

God, who is perfectly just, says that sin is wrong and serious and will not go unpunished. Why? He loves us and treats us seriously. He hates our rebellion against his kind and generous rule. He hates the way our selfishness has wrecked relationship with him and with each other. It breaks his heart to see the hurt we cause to each other.

We may shrug our shoulders, but he can't stand it.

We can't ignore it and we can't fix it

I was surfing one afternoon when my surfboard flicked back and hit me in the face, peeling back my left nostril. I wanted the problem just to go away. What an annoying interruption to a pleasant afternoon in the water. I had things to do and an appointment to keep that evening.

I came running out of the water with blood streaming over my mouth and chin. I tried to assess the damage by looking cross-eyed down my nose. I ran up to a man sitting on the beach and asked how bad it looked. The poor guy went a funny colour of greyish yellow. He turned away saying, "Oh mate, that is really bad."

What was I to do? Ignore it? Push the flapping nostril back into place, apply pressure and hope for the best? Borrow a needle and thread and do a self-stitch job in front of the change-shed mirror? Or go to hospital and have the delicate surgery that would make it right? I went straight for the doctor!

There is only one thing to do with the problem of sin. Go to the one with the expertise to deal with the problem. Go straight to Jesus.

He fixes our problem

Our sin deserves no less than the full weight of God's justice. We deserve the punishment of being separated from God for all eternity. Hell. A real place where there is no love, no trust, no friendship, no good thing because God is not there.

But the astonishing thing is that Jesus, the one without sin, takes the punishment our sin deserves. As Jesus hangs on the cross, the Father withdraws himself from his only Son. Jesus takes the full fury of hell. Earth stood still. Heaven held its breath. In this eternity-shaping action; in this profound, victorious cry, when Jesus says, **"IT IS FINISHED"** we see God's justice done, God's love demonstrated and God's glory displayed.

The death of Jesus is God's astonishing solution to our desperate problem.

He pays my debt

I've joined the cashless society and put nearly every purchase on credit card. But judgment day comes once a month when the itemised bill hits the mailbox. My heart sinks as I scan the list of purchases to that terrifying bottom line. Most I remember. Some I've forgotten. But the bill must be paid. I am responsible. What a relief it is when I make the final payment and the debt is cleared.

For a number of years I had lunch each Wednesday with a workmate. When we ordered our lunch and the waitress gave us our bill my mate would get out his wallet, open it up and show me that it was empty. He'd smile and say, "Oh Dave, wouldn't you know it? Broke again!" This happened so often it became a joke. He was in debt and I had to bail him out. I tried it on him a few times too!

We owe a debt to God that we cannot pay. Jesus' cry, **"It is finished,"** means that the debt is paid in full.

He takes my punishment

I was having coffee with a friend one night and he asked me if I remembered the rugby game we played in together on the previous weekend. How could I forget! I was still wearing the scars of battle. Our opponents had a very aggressive pack of forwards and in every ruck and maul I was the focus of their foul play.

Alan said he could see the 'punishment' I was taking and tried whenever he could to get to the rucks and mauls ahead of me so that he could absorb some of this punishment. It was a small but loving gesture and I was touched by it.

Jesus has taken the punishment that every human being rightly deserves for rebelling against God. Out of his astonishing love for us Jesus has taken the full force of that punishment.

My debt he paid and my death he died. The

punishment of hell he suffered. Why? That I might live.

Victory clinched

I've seen some great sporting victories in my time—most of them on the TV from the comfort of the lounge.

I've also heard great cries of victory, not only on the sporting field, but also in the maternity ward, outside the exam room and at the end of a near perfect wave.

But there is no victory shout like this one. This is by God, for us. This says forever that God is for us. That sin and death are defeated.

This is the greatest victory of all. It is for the whole world. This is a victory where the only losers are the ones who refuse to embrace it and rejoice in it.

No room for resistance

Where does this leave the thinking that sin is a small matter? It required the death of God's Son! What does that do to the self-reliant idea that we can deal with the problem ourselves? Would God have focused the penalty for sin on his only Son if there had been a way we could have fixed it?

There's a chilling exchange between the two main characters in the movie *The Molly Maguires*. A 'mole' befriends, then blows the whistle on a worker who has been sabotaging a mining operation. The saboteur is arrested and sentenced to death. On the day of his execution they meet again in prison.

> "Why did you come to visit?" the prisoner asks.
> The mole responds, "Let's just leave it that I came."
> "No," says the prisoner, "You came for

penance. You want to be set free for what you did."

"But I'm not that soft," the mole replies.

"I don't mean forgiven. You can get that from a woman," says the prisoner with a smile and adds, "You want punishment. You think that punishment will set you free for a brand new life." He then attacks the mole and says, "No punishment this side of hell will free you from what you did."

The mole coldly replies, "See you in hell then."

There *is* no punishment this side of hell that can deal with our rebellion. But Jesus has gone there. He has suffered it so we don't have to. Through him we can be forgiven. It would be lunacy to ignore that provision!

The crucial question

There is a small, historic cemetery in the grounds of one of the churches at Kiama. Just seven graves. One is that of Lt John Gowen, a crew member of the first fleet that sailed into Sydney harbour in 1788. John Gowen's epitaph reads:

Strangers, friends as here you see, the sad truth of mortality. Let each one ask himself: "Am I, prepared, should I be called to die?"

Are you, am I, prepared to stand before our God? How insane it would be to think that trying to live a good life or being a hard worker will make us right with God. No amount of effort can undo the damage we have done to our relationship with God.

But Jesus has dealt with the problem of sin. Our only hope is to trust him.

John 20:1-9

Early on the first day of the week, while it was still dark, Mary Magdalene went to the tomb and saw that the stone had been removed from the entrance. So she came running to Simon Peter and the other disciple, the one Jesus loved, and said, "They have taken the Lord out of the tomb, and we don't know where they have put him!"

So Peter and the other disciple started for the tomb. Both were running, but the other disciple outran Peter and reached the tomb first. He bent over and looked in at the strips of linen lying there but did not go in.

Then Simon Peter, who was behind him, arrived and went into the tomb. He saw the strips of linen lying there, as well as the burial cloth that had been around Jesus' head. The cloth was folded up by itself, separate from the linen.

Finally the other disciple, who had reached the tomb first, also went inside. He saw and believed. (They still did not understand from Scripture that Jesus had to rise from the dead.)

16

About Jesus' Resurrection

I never had the chance to meet my grandfather on my Mum's side. He died before I was born.

I'm told he was a big, happy man who adored his family. They lived in Sydney's northwest, midway between two railway stations. When Mum started work, she would catch the train home from the city with him each day. They could walk from Meadowbank station or stay on the train and catch a bus from West Ryde.

For a bit of fun, they would often have a race, with Mum running home from Meadowbank and her Dad going on to West Ryde and catching the bus. One afternoon Mum arrived home first and waited eagerly for his arrival. Minutes ticked by. Finally a man came bearing tragic news. Between the two stations, David Gallaher had suffered a massive heart attack. He was pronounced dead on the platform of West Ryde station.

Mum was taken to identify the body. Her older brother was away at the war. It was 1941 and she had just celebrated her 18th birthday.

The scandal of death
You can get a real insight into a community's history just by browsing the headstones and reading their

epitaphs. I often wander through the local cemetery of a town or village I happen to be visiting.

Such an activity is not without its lighter side. I've heard of a couple of epitaphs that go like this:

> Here lies the body of Sir John Bristol.
> Accidentally shot by his butler,
> while cleaning his pistol.
> (then below a space on the headstone)
> Well done good and faithful servant.

> Here lies the body of Lester Moore.
> Shot in the chest with a 44.
> No Les. No Moore.

But most epitaphs are not like that. They will tell of a drowning accident where several family members perished together. A mother and a newborn child who died together during childbirth. A mining disaster that claimed the lives of many of the village's breadwinners.

Epitaphs read like poetry. A man's devotion to his wife. A family's love for their father. Some reveal utter despair. Others, a quiet hope and confident trust.

Whichever way you look at it, death is a scandal. It brings to an abrupt end the hopes, dreams and aspirations of the young, and the maturity, wisdom and contentment of the old. It has no respect for age, families or friendships. It's a blight on all that God declares to be good. It makes a mockery of life itself.

Every death is a loss. All of death is a tragedy. The fact of death is a scandal.

A strange confidence
One of my closest friends died recently. That he was 85

didn't make his death any less a tragedy. That he was bedridden for the previous 11 months, due to a stroke, didn't make his death any less a loss. He was God's creation. He was my friend. Now he is dead.

But George lived with a strange confidence, shared by Christian people all over the world. He knew that death was not the end. It was the moment of a new beginning.

Fifteen years earlier, his wife, Peggy, had died. I spent the evening of her death with George sitting at their kitchen table drinking a bottomless pot of tea. I listened spellbound to stories of their life. Early years in the bush. Moving to a busy industrial city. Their courtship and marriage, family life, community and church involvement. We laughed and cried and at the end of the night, prayed together.

As I rose to leave, George saw me to the door. I will never forget his parting words:

> This is a really hard time but in the midst of my grief, let me tell you what I'm sure of. Because of Jesus, Peggy is now in heaven. Because of Jesus, I will soon be in heaven. I just want to give the rest of my life encouraging others to trust in Jesus so that they will be there too.

How can Christians live, and die, with that sort of confidence?

John records the facts

At the conclusion of Chapter 19 John tells us that two men named Joseph and Nicodemus take it upon themselves to bury Jesus' body. Joseph negotiates with Pilate for the body's official release. Nicodemus provides the burial spices (19:38-42).

135

John tells us one other thing about each man, both of whom are highly regarded citizens. Joseph has been following Jesus in secret (19:38). Nicodemus is the same religious leader Jesus challenged (John 3) with the need to be 'born again' (19:39). Is John signalling that both of these men are moving out of the dark shadows of fear, uncertainty and indecision to identify with Jesus?

In Chapter 20 John records the stunning details of Jesus' resurrection. He describes what the disciples discovered on the first day of the Jewish week.

In so doing he lays before us the proof for the resurrection.

I'm using the word 'proof' in the sense of historical evidence for the bodily resurrection of Jesus. There are three main areas of evidence. Let's look at each in turn:

The testimony of his followers

Firstly, there is the eyewitness account of those who saw Jesus alive again. This eyewitness evidence is substantial and conclusive. We are not talking about a 'one-off' sighting in the dying light.

Many people saw him at different times and places. These people knew him throughout his ministry and could verify that the man they saw alive was the Jesus they knew before his death. In John Chapter 20 we have a sample of that large number of people who saw the risen Jesus with their own eyes. He appeared to Mary (20:10-18), to most of the disciples (20:19-23), and then to the disciple Thomas (20:24-28).

Jesus spoke to them, chided them, comforted them, ate with them, invited one of them to prod his wounds, accepted their worship and gave them their ongoing mission in the world. Years later, another New

Testament writer by the name of Paul, said that the facts could be checked out with as many as 500 living eyewitnesses (see 1 Corinthians 15:6).

There is also the evidence of the radically changed lives of these followers. What can account for this change? Only that they encountered their risen Lord who, as he promised, gave them his empowering Spirit.

Peter, who had denied Jesus (see 13:36-38), becomes a man of undying courage. Thomas' unbelief turns to recognising that Jesus is his God. (20:24-28). The story of the beginnings of Christianity, mapped out for us in the rest of the New Testament, show just how dynamic these changed lives were.

Telling evidence at the cross and the tomb

At the cross, the evidence that Jesus was dead is overwhelming (19:32-35). I draw your attention to it because some people try to explain away the resurrection by saying that Jesus was taken down from the cross 'nearly dead' and was able to revive in the coolness of the tomb and escape. The logic being that if there's no death, there's no resurrection.

But John pays careful attention to detail. He shows that the crucifixion was carried out under the strict military supervision of 'crucifixion specialist' soldiers. They ensured that Jesus was dead before his body was taken down from the cross. Jesus was certified dead. His corpse was tightly wrapped with linen and over 30 kg of spices, placed in the tomb, secured by a huge rock and guarded by Roman sentries.

Around 36 hours later there is an empty tomb with revealing evidence both inside and out. It was empty (20:1-8), but the grave clothes were undisturbed. What grave robber in the process of stealing a body would hang around to unwrap and fold the linen?

Outside the tomb, the stone covering the entrance had been displaced, but there were no signs of a scuffle to suggest the guards, crack Roman sentries who would keep post and hold their ground to the death, were overpowered. Theories that the body was stolen can't be sustained in the light of such details.

The trustworthy promises of God

In our eagerness to find reasons and argue for, or against, the evidence for the resurrection, we could overlook what in John's and Jesus' mind is a most compelling reason for believing the truth of the resurrection.

God said he would do it.

The resurrection had been promised in the Old Testament scriptures and Jesus often drew his disciples' attention to those promises. Jesus urged his disciples to trust God at his word. John comments in 20:9:

> **They still did not understand from the Scripture that Jesus had to rise from the dead.**

God, with respect to Jesus' coming, had done what he promised to do.

God, with respect to the resurrection did what he promised to do.

God, with respect to the future and Jesus return, will do exactly what he has promised to do.

When Jesus spoke about his death and resurrection both before and after those events, this is the point he kept pressing. God keeps his every word. He has kept this word. Jesus has been raised to life.

A resurrection world

One of the most difficult aspects of my work as a minister has been to bury people. Sometimes they, and their grieving loved ones, have been all but strangers to me. At other times they are families and friends I have come to know and love. Whether well known or not, it has made no difference. It has been the hardest of all tasks.

The first funeral I took as a minister was a baby who died in her cot. I have never forgotten it. Nor can I forget Nathan, a seven year old, and Philip, in his twenties, who both died within months of each after a long fight against leukaemia. Or Wendy, a vibrant mother of three, whose children, husband and parents cherished her deeply. She died at 35 of cancer. Or John, a close friend, whose untimely death was an awful tragedy.

What hope have I been able to offer these people as they stared death in the face? Or their families as they ached in helpless silence? I couldn't fill their heads with nonsense. I hadn't been on the other side.

But Jesus has.

We live in a resurrection world.

Jesus Christ has come back from the dead. What hope does he offer?

John 20:24-31

Now Thomas (called Didymus), one of the Twelve, was not with the disciples when Jesus came. So the other disciples told him, "We have seen the Lord."

But he said to them, "Unless I see the nail marks in his hands, and put my finger where the nails were, and put my hand into his side, I will not believe it."

A week later his disciples were in the house again, and Thomas was with them. Though the doors were locked, Jesus came and stood among them, and said, "Peace be with you." Then he said to Thomas, "put your finger here, see my hands. Reach out your hand, and put it into my side; stop doubting and believe."

Thomas answered him, "My Lord and my God!"

Then Jesus told him, "Because you have seen me you have believed; blessed are those who have not seen and yet have believed."

Jesus did many other miraculous signs in the presence of the disciples, which are not recorded in this book; but these are written that you may believe that Jesus is the Christ, the Son of God, and that by believing you may have life in his name.

17

More About Jesus' Resurrection

"Blessed are the cheesemakers . . ." is a now famous line from the Monty Python movie *The Life of Brian*. It is, of course, a light-hearted variation of Jesus' words; **"Blessed are the peacemakers . . ."**

Less known, but more hard-hitting, is the variation I heard from a former Australian politician: "Blessed are the cockroaches, for they shall inherit the earth."

With chilling brevity, this outspoken politician dismissed any idea of living with personal hope for what may lie beyond this life. It also ridicules Jesus and the promise of hope he offers his followers in a taunting jibe at that promise.

What lies beyond? Anything? Nothing? I had always thought there were three major views: when you die you simply rot in the grave (blessed are the cockroaches after all); the Eastern view of reincarnation and the Christian view of resurrection. Now I detect a fourth view. I will it call the 'god-slave' view. Let me deal with each of them.

The cockroach view
The cockroach view of life after death is that there is none. This is all there is. It explains life and our origins in purely physical and material terms. When you die you

simply rot in the grave. Nothing more. Nothing less.

Actor Anthony Hopkins summed up this view as he reflected on the funeral service of Sir Laurence Olivier, his close friend and fellow actor. Olivier's coffin was covered in flowers and 'Queen Anne' lace as a tribute to Shakespeare's *King Lear*, and the role that Olivier made his own. As the coffin moved out of view, Hopkins thought:

> So this is Olivier's final curtain. Finally it's all about 'rot'. Nothing lasts really. Darkness and it's all over. Life is a dream. Do you think it will last for a bit?

It's a common view. Ultimately it's all about corpses and cockroaches.

The human being. Born in wonder or neglect. Grows in beauty or abuse. Declines in uncertainty and dies in fear. Then rots or gets torched. Rage against it or resign to it. Some would have us believe it to be true.

However did you notice the trace of longing trailing off in Hopkins' words: "Do you think it will last for a bit?" Can those who embrace it, bear it to be true?

The reincarnation view

The Eastern view of reincarnation has attracted growing interest among Australians and other 'western people' in recent years.

While there are many variations of this view, in essence, it is about coming back to this world after death in another life form—either a higher or lower form of life, depending on your moral performance in the previous life. In its purest ideal, after a number of 'reincarnations' or life cycles of an increasingly higher life form, you reach a point of equality with 'god'.

When I was involved in running a lot of seminars about Christianity in schools, I was amazed to find how many Australian teenagers claimed to believe in some form of reincarnation. Without a shred of evidence for reincarnation, and despite the massive evidence for Jesus' resurrection, they just liked the idea and so embraced it.

Quite apart from the issue of evidence, think about the consistency of this view. If the next incarnation depends on the moral, and even spiritual, performance of the last life, then given the observable nature of humanity, it's odds on that the life cycle will be a downward spiral. We may have much in common with the cockroach after all!

The 'god-slave' view

I am stunned at how easily Australians resort to 'after-life' language in the face of death. It is laughed off as a joke most of the time, but quickly embraced when tragedy and death come close. For want of a label, I call it the 'god-slave' view.

This view has the dead person above or beside us as a kind of god or angel figure, looking down and watching over us. It's a new life form but the focus is very much on our lives and helping us in this life. We are at the centre and they are helping us to fulfil our dreams.

I've heard sailors talk about deceased crewmen being up there putting wind in their sails. Or surfers saying their mates are stirring up the swell for them. Or loved ones acting as guiding and guarding angels.

I don't want to minimise the depth of grief felt by family and friends. But I do want us to think seriously about what is being expressed. Where is the evidence for such a view of life after death?

Look at what else it is saying. The dead are now locked into a phantom-like existence revolving around our lives in this world. It's our self-centredness taking over again as if this life is all there is, or really all that matters, while the poor deceased are seen as slaves to our needs!

The resurrection view

The Christian view of resurrection is radically different. There is genuine historical evidence to back it up (as we saw in the last chapter). Jesus says that those who trust him will be resurrected to life in the age to come with perfect bodies, perfect health, enjoying perfect relationships in a perfectly restored universe.

Life will be as it was created to be before the invasion of sin and its consequences. Far from being the perfect and selfish wish-list that some people like to imagine heaven to be, God will be at the centre and his people will live in happy obedience to him.

Consider carefully your view of what happens when we die. The evidence for Jesus' resurrection cannot be dismissed. It gives us genuine confidence that we will not be cockroach fodder, nor reincarnated to be the cousin of a cockroach, nor left at the edge of the stage of this world endlessly looking on.

Let me turn then to considering what we can be sure of because of the resurrection of Jesus.

Jesus is Lord and God

Firstly it shows us that Jesus is our life-giving God. We can only, and we must, make the same response as Thomas in chapter 20:28 of "my Lord and my God."

In the light of the resurrection we must acknowledge that Jesus is Lord and God. He is the universe's Lord and God. As Lord and God he calls for and deserves our allegiance. His resurrection 'proves' that he can deliver on his promise of life.

The one whom John claimed to be from God, equal with God and God in the flesh (Chapter 1 of the Gospel) demonstrates his 'Creator' power by returning to life.

Think through what this means. In every chapter of John's Gospel, we have met the one who claimed to be God. He backed up those claims with loving displays of God-like, Creator-like power. How? Healing the sick. Feeding the hungry. Raising the dead.

Don't you see that he's itching to do it all over the world, forever? He is Lord and God. He will do it. His resurrection guarantees it.

Sin and death are defeated

Secondly, it demonstrates that Jesus has triumphed over sin and death. His victory shout, **"It is finished."** (19:31) would have been a hollow cry if death had won the day.

But the resurrection is proof and a public declaration that Jesus has paid sin's penalty for his people. He is the only hope for our forgiveness and acceptance with God. His victory over sin and death guarantees a universe where sin and death will be unknown.

Think about what this means for relationships in this 'new creation'. Nothing will hinder our intimacy with God. Nothing will harm our intimacy with each other. Sin is defeated. Our sin forgiven. The reality of sin is abolished. A perfectly restored universe, enjoying perfect relationships—with God and with his people, with perfect 'resurrection' bodies!

Jesus will judge the world

Thirdly, it is clear evidence that Jesus will one day judge the world. His words in 20:29 are decisive:

> **Blessed are those who have not seen and yet have believed.**

They are blessed because of the gift of forgiveness, acceptance and life.

But there is a flipside. Refuse to trust Jesus and there is only the prospect of condemnation, rejection and eternal death.

In the Acts of the Apostles 17:30-31 (the book after John's Gospel in the Bible) we read of this judgment:

> **In the past God overlooked (our) ignorance, but now he commands all people everywhere to repent. For he has set a day when he will judge the world with justice by the man he has appointed. He has given proof of this to all men by raising him from the dead.**

We long for justice. We are rightly outraged when people suffer through the selfish and evil actions of others.

If there is no prospect of ultimate justice, life has no meaning. It has no value, sanctity, integrity or purpose.

The resurrection of Jesus from the dead is living proof that God will bring justice. This risen Jesus will judge the world.

The final interview

The bishop who gave me my first full-time church job was a Welshman who had done some theatre in his younger days. Having celebrity status he was invited to be a guest on a TV chat show.

Lounging on their studio couches, chatting away before a live audience and viewers all over Australia, 'Witty' (as we affectionately called him) broke into the flow of the questioning and asked the chat-show host:

> "Do you realise, that one day the good Lord will be sitting where you are, and you'll be sitting where I am, and you'll be the one being interviewed?"
>
> The TV host responded, "Will it make a good interview?"
>
> "It will be a very short interview," Bishop Witt said, "The good Lord will lean over, tap you on the knee, look you in the eye and ask, 'What did you think of me?' . . . . *and your life will depend on that moment!"*

The resurrection leaves us in no doubt that Jesus Christ rules our world. He is Lord and God. He has conquered sin and death. He will return to recreate the universe as he brings the world to judgment.

Being part of his perfectly restored universe, turns on the issue of our response to him.

PART FOUR

A CHOICE ABOUT LIFE

Chapter 18 looks at the response of faith that Jesus calls for throughout John's Gospel.

John 20:27-29

Then he said to Thomas, "Put your finger here; see my hands. Reach out your hand and put it into my side. Stop doubting and believe."

Thomas said to him, "My Lord and my God!"

Then Jesus told him, "Because you have seen me you have believed; blessed are those who have not seen and yet have believed."

18

About Faith

Friends of mine described their marriage proposal like this:

> "Will you marry me?" he said to her.
> "I guess so," she responded
> "Is that a *yes* ?" he insisted.
> "I think so," she replied.

It wasn't exactly the decisive response he was after! But, ten years on, they are happily married with three adorable and energetic kids. Like marriage, Christianity requires more than just thinking about. It requires action. It requires a decisive response.

The God to trust

To attend the college where I trained for Christian work, I rode a bike through the back streets of inner Sydney. My route took me past a sign outside a church building. The sign read: "God is not an idea to be argued, but a Father to be trusted."

It was a powerful reminder to me each day as I rode on to college to study things about God. Our reading of John's Gospel brings us to the same point.

Jesus is not an idea to be read about. He is the Son of God who is to be trusted.

Jesus himself calls for a response that is described in John's Gospel as belief, faith or trust. It is one of the most popular words in the whole Gospel. This was his very purpose in writing the Gospel. In 20:31 we read:

> **These are written that you may *believe* that Jesus is the Christ, the Son of God, and that by *believing* you may have life in his name.**

The health of relationships

To believe or to have faith or to trust is vital for healthy relationships and therefore to life itself.

I came home from a trip to South Africa a few years ago with a surfboard that I decided to buy there on the spur of the moment. To play a bit of a trick on Helen, I rang before leaving for home, and asked her to put the roof racks on the car before coming to the airport to pick me up. I said that while I was in South Africa I had bought an exquisite African carving that wouldn't fit inside the car.

Helen turned up pretty excited thinking it would be a large carving of a giraffe or some other animal. When I walked through the gate with a surfboard under my arm she was not impressed!

You can get away with a stunt like that once or twice at the most. But if you mislead people you say you love, trust begins to wear very thin.

Trust is the life-blood of relationships. You can trust only what is trustworthy and what is trustworthy is what is true. That is why John has been careful to lay before us the historical evidence about Jesus.

Jesus' call to trust him is based on his absolute trustworthiness. He is the only one worthy of our complete trust.

True and false trust

There is a distinction in John's Gospel between true and false trust. Throughout the Gospel a lot of people's response of trust in Jesus is only shallow.

Many, we are told, **"turned back and no longer followed him"** because his teaching was too hard (6:60-66).

Others would not confess their faith, **"for they loved praise from men more than praise from God."** (12:42-43)

Jesus makes it clear that believing in him and following him involves obeying his teaching (8:31). It means serving him as our Master and serving his people, because he is Lord and Master (12:26 and 13:12-17).

In fact Jesus says we must abandon ownership of our own lives and surrender that ownership to him, just as he surrendered to his Father's will in laying down his life for us (12:25).

In practical terms this will mean saying "no" to our own way and "yes" to Jesus' way for the way we live and the choices we make. This is how we live out our trust in Jesus. This is how we honour him as king. This will often be hard, but worth it and always best for us.

A South African friend, Ross, tells me of a time at a cricket match in Capetown when he heard a stir at the end of the row where he was sitting. He looked around to see Nelson Mandela speaking to an Afrikaans lady in the end seat. She was quite elderly and frail and didn't recognise that it was her president speaking to her.

When she realised her president was speaking to her, she struggled to her feet but President Mandela insisted that she remain seated. She protested saying, "But I must stand. I must stand for my president."

To which Mandela responded, "Well Madam, if I am your president then you must do as I tell you, and I want you to remain seated!"

Jesus is not the president of a country, placed in power for a few years by popular vote. He is the king of the universe, placed there by his Father to rule for all eternity.

To trust him means to do as he tells us and like Mandela with that woman, but infinitely better than Mandela, Jesus rules us in a way that is best for us.

Trust like Thomas

Thomas, the disciple of Jesus, becomes our model of what it means to trust Jesus or to believe in Jesus. Thomas needed hard-core evidence. The risen Jesus stood before him as large as life, and invited Thomas to prod his crucifixion wounds.

For us, twenty centuries later, the evidence is no less compelling.

Jesus won't appear before us as he did for Thomas. But we have the eyewitness evidence of Thomas, John and many others. We have Jesus' promise in 20:29:

> **Because you have seen me you have believed. Blessed are those who have not seen and yet have believed.**

This response of belief or trust is often described in other parts of the Bible as 'repentance'. It means a radical change of mind.

Turning from an attitude of ignoring Jesus, to recognising and honouring him as Lord and God. Turning from self-reliance to relying and trusting in Jesus and his death alone for God's gift of forgiveness and acceptance.

Full speed repentance

When our kids were quite young, we went for a holiday to the Snowy Mountains. We rented a lodge in a village. It was spring and out of the ski season so we had the lodge, and almost the whole village, to ourselves. While there I wanted to walk to the summit of Mt. Kosciusko, Australia's highest peak.

On the day I planned to go I rang the National Park ranger and asked him about the weather. He gave me two pieces of advice for walking in the park. Don't walk alone and do take protective clothing. The kids were too young to take. Helen had to stay back and look after them. I had no adequate clothing. What did I do? I ignored his advice and went anyway.

It was a magnificent day. Fluffy white clouds drifted around a deep blue sky. The sun was warm and there was a light cool breeze. The track was dry, with just a few snowdrifts to scramble over. Streams, bursting with thawed snow, rushed down the valleys. I was a very happy and smug wanderer.

I had ignored the ranger and was getting away with it. What did he know, that joy-spoiling ranger!

Lost in these and other self-satisfied thoughts near the summit, I felt something hit the side of my face. Stunned, I looked up to the west to see a huge hailstorm bearing down on me. It was real. It was frightening. The ranger was right. There was only one sane response to make. Let me describe what repentance looks like at

20 km per hour in a pair of shorts and a light sweater!

There was a small shelter hut down the track. It was my only hope. With large pieces of hail pelting my head and body I headed for the safety of that hut as fast as I could. What wise loving advice that good ranger had given me. If only I'd had the sense to listen to him. It was his country and he knew how it was to be lived in.

Sprinting to the safety of the hut I determined that I would never again ignore and rebel against his advice. This was his mountain and I would live on it the way he knew best for me and others—for our safety and enjoyment.

I had been going my own way, thinking I knew better than the ranger. The first hail strike acted like a warning call. I did a complete U turn and headed in the opposite direction with a new frame of mind, seeking the safety of the hut from the fury of the storm. The hut that the rangers had kindly provided and maintained to save people from perishing!

Jesus calls upon us to change direction, to stop defying him and start obeying him. He wants us to receive the protection against the coming judgment that only his death provides.

Relating to Jesus in this way is the TRUST that Jesus calls for in John Chapter 20. In fact, in the whole of the Gospel! Thomas' words express exactly how every human being must respond to Jesus:

"You are *my* Lord and *my* God" (20:28).

Anything less is not true repentance.

Your response

The reason John has written his Gospel is for us to meet the Jesus that Thomas met. So that like Thomas we may recognise his true identity and give him our trust and allegiance as our LORD and our GOD.

What John asserts about Jesus back at the beginning of his Gospel he now records from the lips of a man who is world-hardened, sin-weary, hope-hungry and seeking the truth. Thomas is just like you and me.

His response, the response Jesus calls for, is to say to Jesus, "My Lord and my God."

A simple prayer that expresses this kind of trust and therefore a person's heart of repentance would go something like this:

> Lord Jesus,
> I turn to trust you as my Lord and my God.
> Forgive me for rebelling against you in the past.
> Thank you for dying in my place.
> Please help me to obey you from now on.

A prayer like that brings the promise and assurance of Jesus of God's forgiveness and the gift of eternal life.

The very life that Jesus came to give to us when he made the promise, recorded in John 10:10, that we have been exploring in this book:

I have come that they may have life, and have it to the full.

Before We Finish

You may be wondering, "Where to from here?"

If you sincerely prayed the prayer I wrote out at the end of the last chapter, or even found your mind and heart crying out in agreement with, "Yes, that's me. It puts into words just where I am at the moment," then you have become a Christian. You have started out on the Christian life.

Like a person just married, you don't have to doubt the reality of what you now are. You are a Christian, a friend and follower of Jesus. Not, 'maybe a Christian' or 'hoping to be a Christian'. You are now a child of God. God's forgiveness and the gift of eternal life are certainties. Again, like one newly married, the Christian life with its joys and challenges stretches out before you.

Remember once again the promises of John's Gospel:

Yet to all who received him, to those who believed in his name, he gave the right to become children of God. (John 1:12)

For God so loved the world that he gave his one and only Son, that whoever believes in him shall not perish but have eternal life. (John 3:16)

I tell you the truth, whoever hears my word and believes him who sent me has eternal life and will not be condemned; he has crossed over from death to life. (John 5:24)

A helpful thing to do at this point would be to seek out a Christian friend and tell them of the step you have just taken. Perhaps the friend who gave you this book, or a Christian you know and trust. They will be able to give you some good tips on how to start out and grow strong in your friendship with Jesus.

You may not be ready to pray that prayer; to take that step and surrender your life to Jesus Christ. If you are in that position then I want you to know that I respect your honesty. I wouldn't want you to take such a step and not mean it.

If something is holding you back, may I urge you to talk to a trusted Christian friend about it. You may not yet be convinced of the truth and trustworthiness of Jesus. Talk about why. Is there an issue in your life holding you back? Again talk to a Christian friend.

Read back over parts of this book that you may have found most helpful. Get hold of a Bible and read John's Gospel through, or another Gospel, say Mark's Gospel, and keep looking into Christianity.

I work for a small outfit called Evangelism Ministries. Our purpose is to help people in their relationship with Jesus Christ. If I, or a member of the team at Evangelism Ministries, may be of any help, do contact us. Write, phone or email us at:

Evangelism Ministries
PO Box A295
Sydney South NSW 1235
Ph: 61 2 9265 1582
email: dofe@ozemail.com.au

Acknowledgements

Heaps of thanks go to the following people.

To my wife Helen and to our now adult children; Jenny, Stephen and Kim. For your support, patience and willingness to allow a window to be opened on some of the fun and more serious parts of our family life in a few of the stories recorded in the book.

To the team at Evangelism Ministries and especially the staff of 2000 and 2001 for help with earlier drafts of this book at our staff retreats. Thanks to Steve Abbott, John Chapman, Greg Middleton, Lesley Ramsay, Stuart Robinson, Sheila Spencer, Dominic Steele, and to our student ministers Tim Bowden, Darren Box, Simon France, Kirsten Hale, Rhett Harris, Carl Matthei and Danny Rurlander.

To friends Mark and Miriam Groves, Chris Hay, Bryan Malone, Gary Millar, Gary O'Brien, Kel Richards and Rico Tice who also gave me very helpful feedback.

To Lyndel Bendall, Mamie Long, Barbara Richards and Claire Smith for their valuable help and advice in editing and layout.

Dedication

This book is dedicated to the memory of two friends, John Turner (1930-1991) and George Piper (1913-1999). These men taught me much about the life Jesus offers.